The Light Bulb Moment

The stories of why we are feminists

Editor: Siân Norris

Crooked Rib Publishing

First published in the UK in 2011
By Crooked Rib Publishing

All rights reserved Sian Norris

Cover illustration by Susie Hogarth for Crooked Rib

Laurie Penny's 'The Female Eunuch: 40 years on' reproduced with kind permission from the Guardian Newspaper. First published 27th October, 2010.

Extracts from Just Women Summer 1992 magazine have been reproduced with kind permission from Dr Sue Tate, and are labelled appropriately

No part of this book, including the cover design, may be used or reproduced in any manner without written permission from the publisher, except in the context of reviews.

978-0-9568985-0-0

Sian Norris is a feminist activist, advertising copywriter and runs Crooked Rib Publishing out of her front room. Born in 1984 in Plymouth, she moved to Bristol at the age of four. In 2003 she went to London to study English Literature and then came back to Bristol again. It was at university that she started writing the Crooked Rib zine, illustrated by Susie Hogarth. The zine evolved into her successful feminist blog, Sian and Crooked Rib, which in turn evolved into Crooked Rib Publishing. She has written for a range of publications, including the Guardian, the F Word, Rockfeedback, The Fresh Outlook and Liberal Conspiracy. When not writing, feministing and working, she watches Marilyn Monroe and Audrey Hepburn movies and reads historical novels as well as some 'proper' books. She cooks, dances and goes to the parks and pubs with her friends. When not doing those things, she is probably on Twitter.

Table of contents

Introduction	10
The Female Eunuch 40 Years on: Laurie Penny	13
Being a feminist: Jane Duffus	18
Dancing naked round bonfires in dead of night: Gillian Coe	21
Skirts vs. Trousers: Jo Swinson	23
From double standards to creativity: Marta Owczarek	24
Boys and Girls: Anna Brown	33
Feminism and Football: Carrie Dunn	36
Taught me a lot about engines, boys and Bullshit: Madeleine Moery	43
Dressing like a lady: Nimko Ali	45
Girls get jam: Shagufta K. Iqbal	47
Mums, bars, books and feminism: Sarah	52
Times and places: Rukshana Afia	65
Peace and justice: Finn Mackay	67
Feminism chose me: Kat Williams	78

Turn your back on page 3: Francine Hoenderkamp	81
Me and that beauty myth: Hannah Mudge	87
Sisters, mothers, daughters: Maria Margarita Terner	94
Questioning gender roles: Rose Clark	96
One reason why I'm a feminist: a confession: John	98
Finding a wider recognition of equality: Jessica Metherington-Owlett	107
In defence of ideas, or, how I became an angry, self-righteous, man-hating bitch: Ray Filar	112
From "fair" to "just": a tale of two Feminisms: Marina Strinkovsky	121
Finding a feminist community: Rose Child	130
Finding my sisters: Siân Norris	134
Inspiring others to their light bulb moment: Lucy Jones	144
Because we should all be feminists: Matt McCormack-Evans	149
It started with a manifesto: Jenny Rintoul	156

Get on the bus: Maureen Beck	162
Working together to switch on the light: Jan Martin	164
The dust was off the doormat forever: Peggy Walker	169
Woman, mother, feminist: Helen Mott	171
Accused of being a feminist: Clio Bellenis	178
Crowing about trauma: becoming and staying a feminist: Debi Withers	181
My story: Natalie Collins	186

Introduction

Sometime back in 2010, the UK feminist website, The F Word, sent me a book to review. It was called 'Click: when we knew we were feminists', edited by Courtney E. Martin and J. Courtney Sullivan and published by the Seal Press. The book was an inspiring collection of stories from women and men who self-defined as feminists and were involved in feminist activism. It is a brilliant book and I would recommend you read it.

And so, an idea was born. We needed this book, I thought, for UK-based feminists. We needed a book that told our stories, and showed the world why women and men in the UK call themselves feminists. A book that shared our experiences, our feelings about, and our love for, feminism. That explained our feminist activism. And that would inspire other women and men to claim feminism as their own too.

I published my review of Click, and gave a call out on The F Word and Twitter to feminists to get in touch and share their stories. The plan was to self-publish an anthology at the end of it.

The replies flooded in. Stories from women and men up and down the country arrived in my inbox, eager to take part in the project. Women and men with different histories, of different ages, who all identified as feminists in unique and fascinating ways.

Some of the stories are funny. Some are moving. Some tell of trauma, some of childhood unfairness. Some are about books that women have read, and people they have met. Some are about mothers and fathers and boyfriends and girlfriends. All of them are inspiring.

Of course, this book is not without its limitations. Because my main source of finding women with stories to tell was the internet, there are gaps. The audience I was speaking to and had access to was already a fairly self-selected group with a range of privileges that meant they were online and social media savvy. I have tried to ensure that the stories are from a diverse group of women and men, and perhaps in the future a follow-up book can be produced with an even wider range of stories and experiences.

I have tried to loosely group stories together so that they are linked. For example, stories about childhood are grouped together. Where this has not been possible I hope there is still a logical and interesting order.

As far as possible I have re-created the stories here as they were sent to me by their writers, bar a few spelling mistakes here or there. This is to respect how some writers change or bend the 'rules' about punctuation and grammar to make a political statement.

The Female Eunuch – 40 years on
Laurie Penny

Forty years ago this month, Germaine Greer's The Female Eunuch was published – and women's liberation would never be quite the same again. Generations of feminists have been inspired by Greer's belligerent, bile-spattered dialectic of rebellion, a 400-page brick slammed through the screen of male entitlement and female submission. At the age of 12, I was one of her youngest devotees, and although today I take issue with many of her conclusions, the book still thrills me to the core on each re-reading.

I spotted a worn copy of The Female Eunuch on my mother's shelf in 1999, and something about the savage cover, showing a hollow female torso with handles hanging from a clothes-rail, seemed to whisper a wealth of dangerous secrets. Like a grimoire in a fairytale, I felt drawn to the book, somehow compelled by it. Leafing through the yellowing pages I realised, with the righteous rage that only a preteen can summon, that I had been lied to. There were other ways of looking at the world. There was more to sex than the sterile, ritualised commercial play my classmates were already rehearsing, more to femininity than the smiling servitude that made my mother and grandmother so unhappy. In later life, I would come to understand this process as consciousness-raising; at the time, it felt like a striplight had been switched on in my mind.

Being a conscientious kid, I immediately got out my best pens to write a letter to Germaine Greer telling her so. Two months later, a package came through the door, containing a postcard with a pair of friendly-looking koalas on it. She had replied! I was in raptures, and vowed to devote my life to feminism. Like any earnest prepubescent convert, I took my devotional text extremely literally. Greer advised all women to taste their menstrual blood in order to combat genital horror – so when my first period arrived, I dutifully did so. It was salty and sour, but not shameful.

Reading The Female Eunuch as a child in the perky "post-feminist" years of Blair's Babes and

Girl Power, I thought I was the only girl alive who still believed there could be more to womanhood than wearing a great dress and smiling for the camera. Well – almost the only one.

In 2001, on a sweltering, sticky coach trip with the local youth orchestra, I was fumbling in my rucksack for a packet of Wotsits when my copy of Greer's book fell out and skidded under the seats. As I scrambled nauseously on the shaky coach floor, I felt a hand on my shoulder.

"Here's your book," said a girl behind me. "Um, are you a feminist?" she said. "I am too. I thought there weren't any others our age." From that moment on, she and I were inseparable. We spent two heady summers sharing secrets, plotting to overthrow patriarchy and holding hands shyly whilst listening to riot grrrl punk on a shared Walkman.

By Greer's standards, we were hardly daring, man-eating sexual revolutionaries, but we wanted to change the world as only teenagers can. Now that I'm grown up, with my own book coming out next year, I know that to create an honest, adult politics of change, one must first interrogate one's idols.

15

Of course, there are problems. As a child, I thought The Female Eunuch had been written just for me – and as it was targeted at bourgeois, well-educated white women living in rich western countries, it practically had. Unlike many middle-class feminists, Greer never claimed to speak for anyone who did not share her background. Unfortunately, the more time I spend with feminist activists, the more I wish she had at least tried. Had strident, second-wave, sex-positive feminism like that espoused in The Female Eunuch been more inclusively phrased, the ghettoisation that still dogs contemporary women's activism might have been avoided.

Another uncomfortable failing of the text is Greer's savage attack on transsexual women. Greer has long led the radical feminist charge against trans women, whom she labels "castrates", fifth columnists mocking real women and invading female space. This is an ugly untruth, and has directly influenced the bitter, childish rows over the status of trans women that still scar the modern feminist movement. Just recently, an angry debate has erupted yet again over whether or not trans women will be welcome at the annual Reclaim the Night march against sexual violence, threatening solidarity among the new generation of activists.

As a child, The Female Eunuch was my bible, but if feminism is to remain a living, breathing, vital movement, we cannot afford to have sacred texts. It is vital that every cohort of feminists remains in a dialogue with its antecedents. Germaine Greer's rage and revolutionary energy resonate across four decades of feminist activism – but we can still question our foremothers, and we should.

Being a feminist

Jane Duffus

I've always had a long-held awareness that life seems less fair for women, which grew into a feeling that too many people were sitting around whinging about this unfairness rather than doing something about it.

So I started to do something, and then discovered a whole world of other people also doing something. And after a while, I realised that what we were doing was 'feminism' and I thought, "OK, I'm happy with that identity" and kept going.

Although I've always had feminist principles – even if I didn't always recognise them as such – if I had to identify a 'click' moment, it would be during a lecture by Professor Lynne Segal at Birkbeck, University of London, when she was discussing her experiences of feminist activism in the 1970s, and the anger she felt at the inequalities women faced. What Lynne was saying made a lot of sense to me, and I ordered her book "Making Trouble" that evening. My activism spiralled from there. While I don't agree with all of Lynne's opinions, I do credit her with focusing me to be the feminist I am today.

Feminism is important to me because the unity and compassion I've found in this community compares to no other I've experienced in my life. Which makes me both sad (that we are such a disparate society these days) and happy (that I have now found so many like-minded individuals).

In Bristol, we're lucky that there is a wealth of thriving, fervent and (unfortunately) thick-skinned people and groups, all working away – sometimes together, sometimes independently – to chip away at the system and try to make a difference to the suffocating sexism of patriarchy which is still stiflingly evident.

Unfortunately, the male-controlled media still likes to portray 'feminism' as a dirty word, one by which they hope you wouldn't want to identify. But I am incredibly proud to call myself a feminist. I've learned a great deal about life and people. I will always be a feminist.

Dancing naked round bonfires at dead of night

Gillian Coe, Just Women magazine

When did I first realise that Feminism ("the advocacy of the rights of women") had relevance to me?

Reading two books in particular – Elaine Morgan's *Descent of Woman,* and Betty Friedan's *Feminine Mystique* – opened my eyes, and things I had known for years, but not acknowledged or put into words before, suddenly sprang into view. It was like knowing your room in the dark, but when you switch on the light, you can SEE it.

Light, I have found, does not always bring joy – more likely astonishment in this case. I have always believed that women are as valuable and intelligent as men, so when I saw that they were treated as less so, and excluded from all manner of things for no good reason, I naturally thought that this should change. It's not FAIR! I thought. It's not RIGHT! I concluded. How can something as patently true as this be denied and ignored? Are they blind, or what?

If you try to talk to those still in the dark, they shy away – "You're not one of those Feminists, are you?". So many people are appalled by the word, as though it implied dark evil doings, probably dancing naked round bonfires at the dead of night and then flying home on a broomstick. Grow up children, fairy story time is over.

Summer 1992

Skirts vs. Trousers
Jo Swinson, MP

My first experience campaigning against gender inequality was at school. I couldn't understand why girls had to wear a skirt, rather than being able to wear trousers if they preferred, as part of the school uniform. I campaigned in the School Council for the uniform code to be changed, but I remember one of my arguments being rather undermined. I made the case that, in the Scottish winter, trousers were more practical as they were much warmer. The Deputy Head remarked pointedly that they may be warmer than "a very short skirt" – a reference to my attire…I actually didn't even want to wear trousers, I was just annoyed that girls didn't have the option. After I left school the rules were eventually changed, and I've been back to there since to speak to pupils about what it's like to be an MP.

From double standards to creativity
Marta Owczarek

I first sensed something was up quite early on, or rather late, looking at it in a different way: I was already about 14, and that's 14 years of unawareness. I wish someone had given me some Little Book of Feminism when I was a kid, perhaps instead of another Barbie. I loved playing with Barbies, but I also loved Teenage Mutant Ninja Turtles and would dress up as one of them for my birthday or other appropriate occasions. Nobody commented on it, until one day I was found involved in a little fight at school, along with some other kids. We were obviously just playing, but the teacher said: "I can see why the boys were there, but you? A girl? Fighting? Shame on you." I was so scared and embarrassed I just ignored how it didn't make any sense.

But liking and acting out movies that were "for boys" was not nearly as transgressive in people's eyes as what I started doing later. At 13 I asked a boy I liked out. He was completely petrified, which is perhaps understandable, but for some reason it also outraged all the girls in my class. The date was rubbish, and nothing came out of it, but that was entirely secondary - the fact that I orchestrated an innocent trip to the cinema in the company of a boy was reason enough to suspect something was not right with me. That was in June, so the school year ended soon and I'd forgotten about it, and thought everyone else did as well. Next year, people started having parties, and at one of those, someone kissed me. I was surprised, but didn't back off - it felt good, it was exciting and fun but I didn't think any more of it. And then at some different party, months later, I met a friend of a friend who I immediately thought was very good looking, and when an opportune moment came, I kissed him.

Now, that was way too much for others to bear: people started to talk behind my back about how I was easy, how it was embarrassing, how I had no respect for myself. I noticed some friends stopped talking to me, and I didn't really know what was going on until some guy made a rude comment to my face. It didn't really sink in; I thought he was just having a laugh. Then one day I was on a tram crossing the Union of Lublin Square, and then it hit me. I thought, why am I being made to feel awful about it? It's not like I've done anything wrong. I did after all ask the good looking boy out, and he said he would, but just "as friends". That left me feeling a bit down, but not too much - certainly not as much as the weird stuff at school. Later someone told me he did that a lot; just kiss girls at parties, not date them. "That's fine", I thought, "but why are people upset about me, if we're essentially doing the same thing, and nobody seems to be making a big deal about it in his case?" I don't think I had a good idea of what it meant, but that day in the tram, I decided I won't let this get to me, and I'd do whatever I want, kiss however many boys I felt like: that I was a feminist. Then a couple of times when kids were making fun of me, I'd reply "I don't care; I'm a feminist", which looking back is really a bit silly, but in my 14 year old head it meant that I had something to defend myself with, something that would throw people off. I wasn't quite right. I would continue to perform my adolescent sexuality mostly how I felt appropriate, but the sexual double standards and the teasing would not cease.

Gradually other pieces started coming together. I noticed how at family gatherings my grandma, my mum and I were always really busy making and serving food, to the extent that grandma rarely sat at the table with everyone else, but was always bringing more food, taking dirty plates out, or heating up the next course. The three of us would spend hours sat in grandma's tiny kitchen, often quite late on the night preceding the feast, chopping up vegetables for Salad Olivier or crushing butter and sugar together for cheesecake in grandma's clay makitra. It was exciting, as I was allowed to stay up late and help, and fun in itself to learn how to prepare things. But I started noticing that both my grandpas and my dad were never part of it; as we were running around making sure everything was ready, whizzing between the table and the kitchen, my grandpas talked politics and my dad just sat there looking very bored. The political discussions caused everyone a lot of grief because they would inevitably become heated and hateful arguments, but rather than engage in the dialogue, grandma or mum would just shush them at some point, and we'd keep eating in silence.

At some point I started talking back to my grandpas, who were very stubborn in their beliefs ("80% of people just can't think!" was one of the least offensive), and probably never really listened to me, but I thought it was wrong that nobody even tried to contradict them and persuade them to be more open-minded. Mum and dad simply endured it until we were out the door, and I guess the way grandma saw it, the more food she'd give them, the longer they'd shut up for. Or that it was then easier to piss off and do the dishes, rather than have to sit and listen to more of it.

Those things started to make me angry long before I understood what they were really about. In fact for a long time feminism was more of an instinct, a gut feeling rather than theories I'd learn from books (maybe because no-one taught us the slightest bit of that at school). Even though I was obviously more aware of sexism and patriarchy, I was still fairly content to choose my own way where I could, and get angry in silence when I couldn't. I thought I was strong enough to ignore the wider world as long as I could deal fairly okay with my immediate surroundings. I was still a teenager when I got seriously depressed. It took a few years of suffering and moving around a lot, trying to find my own place until I realized I needed help, not another escape route.

I started university again from scratch in London, where I always wanted to live. After managing two full years at one school and in a therapy group, I had to move away again, on a compulsory year abroad. Everyone would tell you it was supposed to be the best year of your life, all carefree and fun, but I found myself completely isolated and crushed again, feeling as though I haven't achieved anything, that I was back in my black hole and it was unlikely I was ever coming out. I didn't want to quit another university, so was adamant to wait it out in the beautiful, lively, sunny city which annoyed me to no end if only because everything about it was a direct contradiction of how I felt in it. Most days I would roll down the blinds, stay in, and watch movies. At some point I saw Looking for Eric (Loach, 2009) and Julie & Julia (Ephron, 2009) in close succession and concluded from both that to get my shit together I needed an icon to look up to. In both the protagonists fared from mediocre to pretty bad, and it was a strong, imaginary presence of a hero that helped them arrive to the end of the movie in a visibly better condition. I was never good with figures of authority or role models - that was the crap they made you write about early at school, and you were supposed to choose the Pope or soldiers who died for the motherland ("If World War II happened today, would your generation be as brave and noble as that of your grandparents?"). Role models were there to make you feel bad about yourself in comparison; they were oppressive rather than inspirational. But in these fairly light films, I saw the protagonists facing their own serious personal challenges with tremendous strength derived from their idols. "Should I also come up with someone like that?", I thought, "Could someone I'd have no real connection to make me stronger?" I was intrigued but clueless, so on my friends-only livejournal I asked: "who motivates you to get out of bed and fuck shit up?"

One friend commented on that post, but she replied with a series of people as well as ideas, like

Kathleen Hanna and veganism, and even though feminism didn't explicitly pop up there, as soon as I saw her response I knew what it was that I was looking for. I watched a documentary on Riot Grrrl and remembered how a few years earlier my friend and I wanted to start a zine, and call it Women, Fire & Dangerous Things. We wanted to call it that after a book by Lakoff, in which he makes a lot of points about cognitive linguistics. One of his examples is Dyirbal, a native Australian language where women, fire and dangerous things are all in the same category of nouns and must be preceded by their own separate classifier. To us, aside from sneaking in a clever reference, it also sounded really badass.

The zine never happened, and although my friend and I now lived far apart, I decided to revive the project immediately and set it up as a collaborative blog, in which we could include even more people. The zine idea was initially to contain our feminist rants, but for the blog I was definitely much more inspired by the idea of simply promoting female activity. At the time I was working on my BA dissertation on local female artists combining images and words, but since in my research I kept discovering awesome women who didn't necessarily use both media, I thought it would be great to write about them on the blog instead. Quickly I started to seek out women and stories for the site specifically, and the more I read and looked around, the more I was fascinated and engaged and energized.

Countless examples of amazing women and what they did wasn't the only thing that got me out of the darkness, but ultimately the blog's contribution to my wellbeing was incontrovertible. I finally took everything that always bothered me seriously, and discovered I wasn't the only one who was keen to oppose and change things. That was really the moment when it all clicked, when I stated with full conviction that I was a feminist and wanted to live by it, that it was "important to promote and inspire female activity, expand the scopes of femininity, dispel stereotypes and cushioned conceptions of perfect equality, and protest against discrimination and stereotypes that fuck with female and human dignity", as I wrote in the introductory post. Not much later I found out about feminist groups, organizations, conferences, activist training sessions and other stuff which made me feel very much part of something bigger than my own little writing outlet.

Nothing else had made me feel so liberated and exhilarated before; not adolescent sexual experimentation, not moving around the world, not getting my hair into dreadlocks at 16 even though my dad didn't want to let me, and the boy I was seeing at the time didn't like it either. Not even when I first dated a girl and discovered I didn't always have to wear make-up or well-fitting clothes to feel comfortable around her. Feminism connected a lot of my experiences together and helped me make sense of them, but also pointed me in an outward direction, towards other people and the bigger picture; it gave me meaning but also stuff to do. Feminism was my new best friend who I knew would never leave me. And the blog was later read by an editor of a magazine who liked it so much she offered me a chance to write for them, and gave me the confidence to be a journalist in my own right. Through promoting the activities of all sorts of wonderful women I ended up finding my own, which gave me way more satisfaction and self-esteem than the prescription drugs.

http://womenfiredangerousthings.blogspot.com

Boys and girls
Anna Brown

I was born in May 1981, my brother November 1982 and my male cousin January 1983. We three are very close in age and as our mothers are sisters, we spent a large part of our childhoods together. Our grandmother (Nanny) would often look after the three of us during school holidays and, on the whole, we all got on well. We'd play imaginative games together, favourites being making dens or playing trains with the dining chairs. As the eldest, I'd often lead the games which I'd like to think were fun for all children, not always just families or armies.

Before my second cousin was born, so before I was seven, my grandparents went away to Germany with their friends and, as kind grandparents often do, they brought us each back a gift. My brother and cousin were awarded a pencil case, with a zip all the way around. Once opened it contained colouring pencils, felt tips, a ruler, pencil sharpener, each in their own elasticated holder. Fantastic! Where was mine, I couldn't wait.

I was given two pink handkerchiefs. The injustice still catches in my throat. Handkerchiefs. And what was I supposed to do with hankies? You can't play with them, you can't create anything with them. You just blow your nose on them. And iron them, if you're my mum. I may have tried to be polite but I couldn't help myself and I cried and cried and cried. How unfair, that these two boys, so much younger than me, who could probably barely make use of such a gift, had these fantastic tools at their disposal and I had glorified tissues!

My Nanny was horrified. Well, boys like things like that, don't they? Girls like pretty things and hankies were the only thing she could find. Not this girl. I wanted colouring pencils, and pencil sharpeners and pens with their own, individual elasticated holder. Fortunately, very fortunately, their friends were still in Germany and I was even able to choose the colour of pencil case - I chose dark green. A week later it arrived and I still remember the joy I felt as now I was the same as my cousin and brother. I could create and draw. And the only reason my grandmother had thought I wouldn't want to do this, was because I was a girl, a female child.

Forward about twenty years, I think I was about 23 or 24 and I was reading the Saturday Guardian. The cover was made up of many small pictures of women. The related story inside was that all of these women had been killed the year before by their male partners. I remember reading it and thinking, "This is terrible. This is awful. Why didn't I know about this before? Why isn't anyone doing anything about this?" Shortly after this an opportunity arose that started me on my path of feminist activism.

Feminism and football
Carrie Dunn

I'll always be grateful to my parents for teaching me that I could do anything I wanted. Typical modern parenting, you might think, making sure that their kids have as many career options open to them as possible, but doing what I wanted to do kicked in much earlier.

Specifically, I wanted to go to football.

My dad is a big sport fan; my mum also takes an interest, so perhaps it was inevitable that I'd catch the bug too. As a tiny toddler I'd memorise the names of players in team photos; I'd recite recent results; I'd read the match programmes my dad brought home. And then I nagged and nagged to be taken to football as well.

My lobbying didn't have an immediate effect. Sensibly, before forking out for match tickets, my parents wanted to be sure that my interest would continue. So after being taken to the occasional game, they finally agreed to buy me a season ticket at the age of eight.

And how I loved it. Every other Saturday, my dad and I would go to the game (via the local sweet shop); when our team weren't playing at home, we'd go and watch the reserves, which had the added bonus of being able to collect autographs.

I was always vaguely aware that not many of my female peers at school spent their weekends at football; still, not many of my male peers did either. Sure, they might have kicked a ball around after school when girls didn't so much, but that wasn't the same thing. I'd talk to classmates about the games I'd seen or the players I'd spoken to, and they would have literally no idea whatsoever what or who I was talking about.

It was when I moved up to middle school at the age of nine that I realised some people didn't think football was a natural or normal preoccupation for a girl. And it was a preoccupation, it really was; I remember biting my fingers raw before an important cup game, I remember sulking when I had to go to my best friend's birthday party rather than football, I remember carefully cutting out match reports from the Sunday papers and sticking them assiduously on my bedroom wall.

I knew how much I loved football, and so did my family and friends; but these new classmates and teachers at middle school didn't quite comprehend. I told the drama teacher that I wouldn't be able to play the role I'd been cast in for the Christmas show because my team had a midweek match that night; in retrospect, she must have thought I was joking until I didn't turn up. I wanted to join in the mass kickaround every breaktime on the school field, and harangued and harangued until the all-male squad let me. Older boys tended to be slightly amused when they heard I was a big football fan, and attempted to humour me; that is, until I challenged them to a trivia contest and invariably won. (I was reminded of these episodes seven or eight years later when, in a pub quiz, my friends and I had teamed up with a couple of older male regulars who we knew by sight but had never spoken to before. When a relatively obscure football question arose, the men were racking their brains; I was adamant I knew the answer, but they refused to accept a teenage girl would have some kind of sporting knowledge they didn't. In the end, I told them to put my answer down and if I was right they could buy our drinks for the rest of the night; if I was wrong, I'd buy theirs. Let's just say my purse remained closed for the rest of the night.)

Maybe I didn't know the word feminist then, but I knew the feeling.

I knew I knew just as much as the boys; I knew I had just as much right to pay my money and go to football as they did; I knew I felt crushed, embarrassed and patronised when people smiled disbelievingly when I told them about my fandom. I'd never felt like this when I was actually at football; so why was it happening now?

Of course, I was encountering explicit gender expectations for the very first time. I was being expected to develop 'appropriate' feminine interests, and dress in 'appropriate' feminine ways, and act out 'appropriate' feminine behaviour. More than that, I was encountering a gender division at football for the very first time. A little girl with her daddy at football is gender-neutral. A teenage girl making her own way to the ground and to her seat is fair game for sexist heckling, apparently. It didn't happen every week, but it meant I was always listening for it, and could never fully relax in a place I had always thought of as 'mine'.

I began to identify as a feminist and use the word to describe myself when I was about 14; as I moved through sixth form and on to university I realised the myriad meanings and connotations of the term, but found that openness liberating rather than confusing. I continued going to football every week (making my own way to a lot of away games by myself after I turned 18) and when I wanted to earn extra cash to pay my way through my English literature degree, it was probably inevitable that I started to write professionally about football – interviewing my team's players for the official website and covering other matches for national sports agencies when my team weren't playing.

Since then, I've made a career of writing about sport. I've reported on World Cups and Olympics, the Premier League and non-league. When Sky Sports' Andy Gray and Richard Keys were recorded off-camera making sexist comments about women in football, my heart sank; can it possibly still be that nearly 30 years after I first went to football a woman must prove herself and her knowledge over and over again in a way that a man never does?

That very question is one of the reasons I began researching the experiences of female football fans for my forthcoming PhD thesis, and yes, it does seem that this still happens. Happily, it also seems that this happens less regularly now than it would have done 30 years ago; indeed, Keys himself has admitted that he and his colleague are 'dinosaurs'.

That's not to say that football is perfect. The fact that FIFA, the sport's world governing body, has a committee populated by a bunch of late-middle-aged white men is indicative of just how far there is to go; ditto the distressing sight of 'cheerleaders' on football pitches at half-time, or the scantily-clad Soccerettes on Sky Sports' Soccer AM, or cameramen's irritating penchant to cut away from action on the pitch to an attractive young woman in the stands.

But it's getting better, thanks to the increasingly visible women in the British game – people like West Ham's chief executive Karren Brady, also known for her role on BBC One's The Apprentice; television presenters Gabby Logan and Georgie Thompson; commentator Jacqui

Oatley; and high-profile professional players like Faye White and Kelly Smith. In a world where football is the fastest-growing participation sport for girls and young women, their fandom and knowledge is finally acknowledged, accepted and welcomed. And perhaps somewhere right now a teenage girl is winning a wager with a bunch of men because she knows the right answers in the sports round of a pub quiz.

Taught me a lot about engines, boys and bullshit

Madeleine Morey, Just Women magazine

For as long as I can remember, I have held broadly feminist views, and even at school I pushed for the girls to be allowed to do a car maintenance course in the dinner hour. (And very interesting it was too; taught me a lot about engines, boys and bullshit).

But, oh, I admit it, I did not call myself a feminist. Not that is, until one winter's day about ten years ago, when my friend Sue Watling and I were supping at my kitchen table, and I happened to say that I thought some feminists were a bit extreme and did women no favours.

That did it! For the next quarter of an hour, I was privileged to be on the receiving end of the

Watling Lecture on Feminism. In fifteen minutes, she covered the Women's Movement Past and Present, Current Objectives and Stereotypes Invented by a Hostile Media. "And what is more," she went on, "in order to move society one inch in the right direction, someone has to be pulling it from about a mile ahead. That is what your so-called extremists are doing".

She was right, of course. Cheers, Sue!

Summer 1992

Dressing like a lady

Nimko Ali

I think I was always a feminist, but it took time to say it out loud, I am from a community that believes women are secondary to men and should be seen and not heard and all that BS stuff. I remember as kid being told what I should wear, think and believe as a woman. But moment that I found my voice as a feminist was when I was 13 and local holy man as he called himself, saw me with my mum and started talking at her about me and how he thought I should dress like a lady and not a boy in pants. And I just remember the words coming out of my mouth. "Who do you think you talking to, and what does what I wear matter to you". And I remember the look on my mums face; it was horror at me standing up for myself to this fool.

Who believed having 3 wives was ok and education was not needed for girls.

And that was when I came out as a Feminist. But deep down I know my mum was and is one in her own small way, but stepping out-side of the frame-work that is hard in our culture!

Girls get jam
Shagufta K. Iqbal

Jam is for Girls, Girls get Jam

But we awoke to the sizzle of eggs in the pan
I liked mine well done and my sister liked hers with the yoke just so.
Yes, we were girls, but we got eggs not jam.

BUT: we were made to know:
I was not born boy
I was not born to be man
I was born to be given away
And that's why girls get jam.

And that is why I have not one but three beautiful sisters

because I was not born boy.

And I was made to know that:

I escaped the desert sands

my mouth was not placed over with hand.

I was lucky enough to born after the gift of the Qur'an

to be protected by the word of Allah

and still my Ummah does not hear the compassion of Allah

still my Ummah chooses not to see the light bestowed upon us by Allah.

Yes, bones lie scattered criss-crossing through the deserts

under the feet of our beloved prophets.

And like my mother the desert heat suppresses secrets

and mass graves gather under sand dunes.

No, I cannot tell you why that girl child

Buried breathing lies in the embrace of the Sahara.

And yes, I must cover.

Live enshrouded.

Black cloth grazing against my skin,

protecting me from everyone else's sin.

My face, my eyes, my lips, my words and my honesty.

And yes, I must pluck, and wax, and tweeze, and squeeze, and polish,

and lipo, and SMILE, full lips, big tits, designer vagina.

Because this way it gets called freedom.

My identity and my honour lie not in me

but in those who own me

And oh how they adorn me

I tinsel like Christmas tree

purple bruises sparkle against my face.

You see in the land of the free,

by the man I love

I am battered every 15 seconds,

and in the land of democracy I was only given the right to speak in

1918

or shall I say 1928.

Sssssssssssssssssssssssh, yes he said hussssssssssssssh,
Because only in 1991 did it become rape,
So don't say a word he says.
But I, I just have to ask: is that why even today
only 4.2% of rape cases lead to conviction?
Yes, they all just let him walk away.

Because I was not born boy,
I was not born to be man.
I was born to be given away.
And that is why girls get jam.

AND they call us traitors
we give away land
we do not carry our fathers names
we disappear in family trees
no one can trace who we are
there is no leaf left for me.
And as silent as sweltering heavy nights
we are considered to have come from thin air
giving birth to strong sons

serving great husbands
burning to death on funeral pyres.
The Ganges just rolling on by
unperturbed by that smell of burning flesh
the stench of charred hair
that once tumbled down a honey brown back.

And they remind us,
we got lumbered with jam
we were born to be given away
and no one loves those
who aren't here to stay.

Mums, bars, books and feminism
Sarah

I'm a cis, straight woman, from quite a middle class background. I currently work in the public sector in a job I love, earn around £17,000 a year, am single and rent a house with a friend. I would categorise myself as Marxist Feminist.

I came from quite an unusual for the time family in that my dad brought me up whilst my mum stayed at work. There wasn't any hidden dark secret reason for it; my mum earnt more than my dad in a job that she loved, she wasn't particularly maternal (a fact she admitted to me on more than one occasion) and whilst she was the youngest in a small family, my father was the eldest of five, and had practically brought his younger brother and sister up. It made sense for him to give up his part-time job to look after me, and then my sister who came three years later.

Being a stay-at-home dad was tough in the early eighties. My dad faced a lot of discrimination, as it was presumed by most of the organisers of activities for young children that they would only be dealing with mothers. The first time I was in my local paper was when my father sued the local swimming baths after we were turned away from galas and mums and tots events because he was a man. Apparently the other mothers felt uncomfortable being around a man, only seeing the difference in genders rather than the fact he was a carer for a young child who was thusly discriminated against. Whilst many parents would have given in, my father refused, and the council was forced to change its policy.

By the time my sister was five the council had a dedicated equalities team and there was absolutely no service for parents and children that catered exclusively for women. I had been brought up not just to see inequalities and disapprove of them, but to seek them out and fight for them to change.

My mother wasn't particularly political, or at least if she was she never spoke about it. What she did have however was an overriding sense of what was "right" and "proper". My life was lived using strict guidelines; you worked damn hard because you were clever, and stupid people were not worthy of your time. You argued your case, spoke up in class, read everything, knew what was happening in the wider world and never ever ever let your guard down. How other people saw you was everything.

Her mother had been a bit of a Victorian and she carried some of these values to her daughters. We didn't wear make-up, make-up was for common girls, and if you wanted to look "nice" you wet your fingertips and smoothed down your eyebrows, which you never plucked. There was no point in shaving your legs; nice girls didn't wear skirts without tights.

I was incredibly conscious of the hair under my arms, every picture of women I saw were smooth hairless freaks, so I secretly shaved them, hiding the razors in my room along with my secret stash of thongs and tampons. I desperately cared about what people thought of me because I was an unattractive, flat-chested swotty teenager who went campaigning for a minimum wage on the weekend. I wore thongs because magazines (that I would steal off friends, not being allowed them at home) used the phrase "VPL" and my girlfriends adopted it and I became terrified of my knickers. I would literally hand wash my own knickers in order for my two worlds- my mother's of "if you wear thongs you're a slut" and my friends "if you can see your knickers through your trousers you're a slut" not to collide. All the time, that was what you were, it didn't matter that you'd never even kissed a boy; you were a slut.

All this came to a head with my mother with the tampon war. For some reason my mother believed, mistakenly, that you could only use a tampon if you had had a baby. I'm guessing this is because that's what she had experienced. I hated (and still do hate) pads, as they combined a lumpy mass of cotton wool and blood with my overriding fear of people seeing my knickers. I started using tampons about nine months after I started my period, when I was twelve. Knowing that my mother didn't use them, had never bought me them and had never mentioned them, and that this usually meant they were a "bad" thing, I bought them myself with my pocket money, hid them and the mess in my room and prayed for the toilet to never block.

Then my sister started her period. I indoctrinated her into the secret tampon stash when she brought it up that she wanted to use them. All went well until about a year later, when I was sixteen, when she called into the living room asking me if she could borrow one as she'd run out. My mother overheard and hit the roof. She tore up to my room and emptied out all my drawers looking for "evidence", finding not only a box of tampons and three pairs of thongs, but the two-pack of condoms my school had given everybody for free during PSE.

That was it; I was a Slut, not fit to be around normal decent people. I had no shame, I was a wicked influence on my sister, I was a whore, no wonder my GCSE grades were predicted to be so low (I had then undiagnosed dyscalculia, and was achieving As and A*s in everything except Maths and Physics. To my parents this meant I was a delinquent). That was the only time my mother ever hit me. I went into the box of tampons and showed her the information sheet explaining that even virgins (like I was) could use tampons. She had never had any of this explained to her; a forty eight year old woman in a position of power had no idea about her own body and what it was capable of, and was passing that message to her daughters. I think it was about this point I began to question my parent's strict socialism, and see that the world is divided first by class, then by gender.

Strangely, it was my mother who introduced me to feminism. She gave me a copy of The Woman's Room when I was fourteen, saying that this book had changed her life – like the Fay Weldon quote on the cover said it would. It had made her swear never to clean up a man's piss for no pay. This is the motto by which I still stand; it perfectly combines my Marxist and feminist beliefs.

I read it all the way through about three months after the tampon debacle. I was shocked; why would these women ever allow the awfulness that was being a 50's housewife to happen to them? Then I realised they had no choice, in the same way I had no choice to wear knickers I hated and shave under my arms twice a week. A combination of fear of being socially outcast and it being the routine I had got myself in kept me doing what I didn't want to do. I couldn't imagine an alternative. I still love the book, re-read it at least once a year and must have bought about twelve copies that I have just given to people. The racism it contains makes me baulk, and I wish that someone would produce an edited version so I didn't have to apologise for it being one of my favourite books.

The book that made me feminist, however, was Roddy Doyle's "The Woman Who Walked Into Doors". I studied it for my English A Level. There is a chapter where he describes the main character's school days, where she is constantly called a "slut". Nothing I had ever read resonated with me so much. This was me! This was the situation I was in at school! I wanted to have sex (by this time I was), but why did this make me bad? But if I didn't have sex, or refused to let the boys feel me up I was a frigid dyke! It all made sense; it was like this for everyone.

This is the biggest problem; women don't talk about it. They go through their younger years being bullied, both by girls and boys, for being something they're not and it wouldn't matter if they were and they *hide* it. Magazines used "VPL" as a tool to keep an entire generation fearful, constantly on guard. When you're too busy worrying people can see your pants, you're hardly going to fight for a better wage, are you?

I left home to go to uni when I was eighteen and stupid. The first year, I didn't eat more than a sandwich a day for six months, because all the other girls were so much thinner that I was and I was afraid of that difference marking me out. I am naturally tall, and broad, and big, and most people I was friends with back home were the same. The fact I went to a uni with a dance school in it can't have helped but I was surrounded by very petit, pretty girls whereas I was a 5'10" sab, stop-the-war hunky type, built to get ragged around by the cops, not sit daintily for photo shoots. I took gender studies as an elective and was forced by a Greerite to chant "I have a clitoris" in class, so I never went back.

In my second year I moved to the nearest city, where I still live today. I was broke, and had trouble finding work in the first few months so took a job selling shots round bars in the city centre. This was what made me the feminist I am today, whereas before I had dabbled but concentrated more on the animal rights/pacifism side of things.

My enforced dieting had left with quite an attractive figure. I was a size ten, aged 19, had longish hair for the first time, and my tits had suddenly quadrupled in size. The job (that was in all likelihood completely illegal) involved buying the cartons of shots from my "boss", selling them and giving most of the money back. I think I made about a fiver a box, and could sell maybe two boxes an hour. Not bad money, considering the minimum wage at the time was just under four quid an hour. I soon figured out that if I wore what the others girls were wearing, i.e. not a lot, I made a hell of a lot more money.

Soon I was living a double life. Most of the time I was still my activist-poet-weirdo self. I hated makeup, lived in jeans and baggy t-shirts and had a boyfriend who sold the Socialist Worker. On Friday and Saturdays I became another person entirely, short skirts, my hair done by my pixie housemates (who loved it when I dressed up as I looked "normal"). Tits out, slap on. I raked it in. I could be as flirty as you like with the hoards of men, but still approachable and ugly enough in the face not to be a threat to the women, who all bought the shots off me. The bouncers loved me, and I made a fortune. My boyfriend hated it. He was scared stiff I was going to get assaulted, and hated the clothes and the slap, saying they "demeaned" who I was.

I carried on like this for about six months. I got grabbed a fair bit, and called all sorts of stuff, but I got grabbed and called stuff all the time anyway by police and even fellow activists! (One of my home town's stop-the-war founders was viciously anti-women, the rumour was he'd been chucked off Greenham Common and was bitter about it. He would patronise everything any of us said and say things to other male activists about us only being needed to make the tea and so the cops didn't come down on us too hard. He also called me ugly to my face when I was seventeen).

Then one night, I was on my own. By this time I was "in charge" of a couple of other girls but one hadn't turned up and the other I'd sent home because it was quiet. A group of men came in on a birthday night out and I waited until they had drinks already (never compete with the main bar was the first rule) before I made my approach. I was wearing a short denim skirt and tight white halter neck top.

At first everything was fine; they bought the shots off me and left me alone. Then I went to the loo, which was down a corridor off the main bar. On the way back one of the group approached me, backed me into a corner and said that if I gave his mate a blow job he'd buy the rest of my stock. I told him no; he said "that's what you girls are there for", grabbed me and dragged me out into the main bar. His friend saw, gathered round me and the Birthday Boy pulled out his penis. They were all laughing at me trying to force me to get down, calling me a slag. The bouncer ripped the guy off me and pulled me away. After checking I was alright, he went and got the bar manager. The bar manager told me he was sorry, but he couldn't throw them out as they were spending so much money, the bar was quiet otherwise and that I was causing the problem by being on my own. I left, got the bus home in tears and never went back. I never got that night's earnings and never ever told my boyfriend. I've never actually written any of that down before.

The bars I worked in were next to lap dancing clubs. I later worked as a supervisor in a pub with dancing poles in the windows. The city I live in has more sex encounter venues that any other in the country, bar London. Bar workers earn minimum wage whilst the strippers go home with hundreds, claiming the clients are the ones being used. But it's the bar staff in the regular bars and clubs, and the girls selling the merchandise that get their arses pinched, and they have never chosen to work in the sex industry. Now they're talking about building a Hooters in my city where the women who work there are forced to sign a contract saying they will never sue a client for sexual harassment. The entire city is turning into one big brothel, where most of the workers have never consented to work.

This is my issue; how can you possibly say the sex industry does not encourage men (and women) to treat everyone they encounter as theirs to use as they will? I know full well it does because I lived in it for years. It is only now, that I work away from the service industry; I don't get sexually assaulted at work at least once a week. I *loved* working in pubs, but working in the city centre and being female was tantamount to carrying a sign saying "grope me" most of the time. Counter this with an appallingly low minimum wage and lack of decent public transport after ten o'clock and you have a lot of very poor, very scared women just trying to do a job.

Since the end of uni I have been a Marxist feminist. I read the books, and since the discovery of Twitter: the blogs. I found The F Word website when I was twenty two. Feminism is everything to me. Without it I wouldn't be able to see straight for anger most of the time. The majority of my friends (having left the sab crowd behind) would not call themselves feminist, and one of my best friends is anti feminist. She looks forward to the day when she doesn't "have" to work because her boyfriend will support her. ("He likes having me at home, knowing that he's supporting me", really, and what happens when he leaves you? Or you leave him? Or he dies? Of course I can't say these things to her because "it's all about choice".) If I didn't have Twitter, the feminist safe spaces online (and thank fuck for The F Word, whose anti-transphobic, pro-choice stance has been my saviour on more that one occasion, especially since I had my abortion two years ago) and more recently the feminist network growing in my city I honestly think I would go insane.

It really upsets me when people misrepresent feminism as somehow man hating, or worse, sexist in itself for directing its main impetus on the devaluing of women. This is why I am a <u>Marxist</u> feminist. It is important to recognise there still is underlying misogynies even in a classless system, and these misogynies should be recognised and acted upon. Every day things happen to make me re-evaluate my thoughts and reassess my privileges. A close friend recently came out as self-identifying as female, which has led me to researching Trans issues a lot more; you think there's a glass ceiling for women, well it's doubled glazed for Trans persons!

I still believe what my parents taught me; you seek out inequalities and fight for them to change. Because there's a hell of a lot of women out there giving blow jobs on dance floors who have no idea they don't have to unless they want to, and if they want to it's alright. Never let the bastards grind you down, read everything, know what is happening in the wider world and always, always speak out.

Yours in comrade/sisterhood.

Times and places

Rukshana Afia

The Sudan 1950s, an evening party, we children were sitting under the table, I said I'd rather marry a woman than a man but women couldn't marry each other 'they can in England' came the confident reply from another little girl.

Zurich 1959/1960? My mother buys me jeans imported from America - we later find them unobtainable in England.

Cambridge 1961, my mother's choice of primary school is not a little influenced by the headmaster allowing both girls and boys to wear long trousers at any age.

Cambridge 1967/8, discovered at 14 reading Simone de Beauvoir's "The Second Sex" when I should have been working on future 'O' levels my mother begins to remonstrate then leaves me to it. 'I suppose it's part of your education'. Later she orders 'Women & Socialism' especially for me from London.

Cambridge 1969/1970. My best friend rings to invite me to join Cambridge's 1st women's liberation group. I decide that 'O' levels are more important (!)

Halifax 1970/1. The day "The Female Eunuch" comes out my mother and I buy it immediately for each other.

Bristol 1972, I join the Student Union WLM group and read everything I can find, buying most of it. Finally, once dropped out I join the local movement (many groups) and feminist activism starts for me.

Peace and justice
Finn Mackay

Incidentally, I think the question 'when did you realise you were a feminist' is a very hard one for people to answer, in my experience lots of women say they have 'always been' a feminist, like it is biological or something, but they can't actually specify when they started to identify as a feminist, let alone why.

I'm not sure I can remember when I specifically started identifying myself as a feminist to people. I was aware of the word as a child because my Mum ran a local women's group in the rural area of Scotland where I grew up. I remember my Dad would have to go into the loft and watch the black and white telly while the women's group polished off his homebrew downstairs and got increasingly raucous! All around reviewing Greer of course and various other intellectual and consciousness-raising pursuits I'm sure! She had feminist books in the house, and copies of Spare Rib. I do remember telling people as a child that I was a feminist, and I thought sexism was when men tried to get sexy with women when they didn't want them to, like flirty or gropy men!

I think I first got a political understanding of women as a group and as a political group though, when I became aware of the women's peace protest at Greenham Common. Two women who went to Greenham lived in the next village from us and they were friends with my parents, so we used to go to parties at their house. They were very cool, they had a van, they told stories of living in tents and getting arrested and sitting up late round fires singing and laughing, and I was completely inspired by the whole thing. I wanted to go to Greenham from the age of 7. When I was about 8 or 9 I was a regional finalist in a South West Scotland Peace Song Contest, with my song 'Join Hands Around The World' about the women of Greenham Common! And I used some 'puff paints' that I got for Xmas to design myself a Greenham Women's Peace Camp tee-shirt! I was obsessed, I listened to tapes of Greenham peace songs and learnt all the words!

I was quite political generally as a young person, I became vegetarian when I was 12 and used to do a display in our school library about animal rights. I joined the National Anti-Vivisection society and Compassion in World Farming. I organised a sponsored walk for NAVs and wrote letters to the local paper against fox hunting and vivisection. I used to take the NAVs Animal Defenders merchandise catalogue into school and get peers to buy stationary and pens and badges from them, and then I'd take their money and send it off and get the order and then take their things into school for them.

I read some of 'The War Against Women' by Marilyn French, which I thought was good. So obviously by then I knew a bit more about what the word feminism meant and what sexism was, and I was telling school friends that I was a feminist and that this meant I thought women should be equal to men and should be able to do things as women and could do just whatever men could do and should feel powerful and strong.

Then when I was 17 and left school I waited until my parents were out, as I wasn't allowed to use the phone, and I rang directory enquiries and got the number for CND, and I rang them and asked if there were any permanent women's peace camps left in the country. They told me about a women's peace camp outside the American military base Menwith Hill in Yorkshire and I rang the contact number and arranged to go there the next week to stay for the summer holidays. I had never been on a train by myself and had to go to Carlisle, then Leeds, then Harrogate and get picked up there by women from the camp. Lucky for me I arrived at camp while the women were on the Women on the Road for Peace tour; so I went with them to Sellafield and Aldermaston and then Greenham Common! I couldn't believe it; I couldn't believe my luck, ten years later to get to go to Greenham. I was so moved. It was hilarious really that I was such an anorak, when women were singing songs round the fire and forgot words or verses I was there going 'ah, no, I think you'll find the next verse is actually 'woman tiger, woman dove, help to save the world you love' then 'iron fist in velvet glove'....' !!! They thought it was hilarious, as they were all Greenham women and I'd never been, but I knew all the songs!

That experience of being in a women-only space, of seeing women doing everything, living outside successfully, organising political campaigns, running court cases, doing media work and public speaking and writing articles; it was so inspiring and empowering. I met so many amazing and impressive women, I wanted to be as brave and forthright as them, I wanted to make things happen. I thought women could do anything and worked very well in a group on their own without men. I got arrested! Which was really scary the first time. But I felt proud. The main thing I was impressed with was how welcoming the women were and how they were not patronising at all. I was only 17, I didn't even know what Menwith Hill the military base was or did, but the women included me in everything from the start. I was involved in the circle meetings like everyone else and asked for my opinion on decisions about things and it was so wonderfully inclusive and non-patronising.

Anyway, so all of that just furthered my identification with feminism, and I was very aware that peace is a feminist issue and I saw the protest as a feminist campaign. I saw it as a counter, and a visible statement against the patriarchal militarism of the base. I saw how the women worked together in solidarity and in unity and sisterhood and in a really creative way, doing great and creative actions with so much humour; it was such a laugh. And I thought what a difference that was compared to the military and police on the military base and how they worked in such a male and linear and hierarchical patriarchal way. They really didn't know how to respond to our crazy, creative actions!

Then I went to agricultuaral college, but spent every holiday at the camp at Menwith Hill. And when I finished my course I went to live at the peace camp, getting involved in everything, writing newsletters, doing public speaking tours and media work, getting arrested, defending myself in court, organising direct action protests, living outside! I did that for about a year and a half, before I went to live with my first girlfriend and her mum.

Her mum happened to be one of the women who started the Reclaim the Night marches in the UK in the 1970s and an influential second wave feminist - Al Garthwaite. I was very impressed with tales of 2nd wave feminism, and direct action. Through her I met lots of other inspiring 2nd wavers and Radical Feminists; then Julie Bindel came to lodge with us while working on the Violence, Abuse & Women's Citizenship Conference in Bradford in 1996. I was volunteering for that at the admin office, as well as for the feminist archive. I was getting totally into radical feminism; I met Emma Humphreys, and anti-prostitution campaigner Fiona Broadfoot. I don't know why, but I immediately identified with Radical Feminism, I immediately thought that male violence against women was the big issue, the keystone of our oppression.

I was very inspired by Julie Bindel when I first met her. I was impressed by her work with Justice for Women and her unapologetic and angry feminism. I'm very pleased that she is still a good friend, comrade and sister, and she remains a constant inspiration. But anyway, I identified immediately with Radical Feminism, though I also had a lot of more lefty women around me, and socialist feminists. I felt that women had a right to be angry, I was angry for myself and for all women, I was outraged at violence against women and outraged that nobody seemed to care and that feminism was a fringe and isolated movement, rather than a huge, mass movement in the country as I thought it rightfully should be. Then I saw Andrea Dworkin speak at the conference and got to meet her afterwards, and that was incredibly inspiring. So, by that time, in my late teens, I was identifying as a Radical Lesbian Feminist.

I was still involved with the peace camp, but doing more work on the theoretical side of why peace is a feminist issue. At this time, I was still sorting out my own court cases and fighting several of those, and doing talks about the peace camp around universities. I was working with Helen John, who I first met when I went to Menwith Hill. She was one of the founders of Greenham Common and is another source of inspiration for me and one of my heroines. Again, another unapologetic, committed and certain woman, sure of her beliefs and actually putting them into action and making things happen, on her own if need be.

When I was about 22 or 21 I went to university to do women's studies, and actually entered a very un-political period of my life, as, at that time, university was very post-modern and quite anti-feminist! I did a Gender Studies masters after that in London, and got involved with the Emma Humphreys Memorial Prize while living there. I had been doing volunteering since undergrad at Citizens Advice Bureau and then in advice centres; then I went into work as a youth worker; then doing adult advice work with men mainly, prison leavers and adult returners to work and training, homeless guys etc. After that I joined a Local Education Authority, starting and running a domestic violence prevention project in schools in North London and did the local government thing for a few years before returning to education ten years later and am now doing a PhD. But while doing all that I was still doing activism, peace stuff with CND and Women's International League for Peace and Freedom and Women in Black vigils now and again.

In 2004 I founded the London Feminist Network, frustrated that there didn't seem to be much feminist activism going on, in the grassroots. Unless you were working in an agency, or service provider in the women's sector, there didn't seem a way to get involved, and also everything seemed to be online, nobody met face-to-face.

Based on my grounding in the women's peace movement I felt it was vital to meet face-to-face and get inspiration and solidarity from one another and plot great direct action and events and stunts and make them happen together. So that was my motivation for starting the group that summer. I organised a conference that year too, on women's rights in London, inviting women I knew from the peace groups; as well as Trade Union groups and anti-racism groups who I had met through my lefty work, membership of Unison and CND activism.

Then we organised a Reclaim The Night. I'd been wishing that could happen again, as the conviction rate for rape was worse than it was when the marches were first started and I thought: we need this march again! We need to bring these things back, we need a revival! A feminist revival. A colleague from the Lilith Project said they could help with photocopying flyers and publicising it, so we both thought, let's just do it this year, in November on the UN day to end violence against women (25th) and the new LFN could call it and organise it.

Even though this was only a few weeks away from when we made the decision to go with it, we thought we'd go ahead anyway. And we got about 30 women. I painted an LFN banner and bought poles from B&Q and took it along and we had a presence and it grew from there. Then the next November I organised the march again, doing a lot more work on it and planning it a lot further in advance, and cycling around London dropping off flyers and talking to people at any events at all to do with women! And we got 500 women on the next one, and then it grew and grew.

It caught a vibe I think, women were looking for something to get active and involved with. The timing was right and LFN grew too, from about six women to now around 1500. And of course we get over 2000 on RTN march every year, with women even travelling from Europe to attend.

Anyway, this has turned more into a life story than how I became a feminist! But there you go, that's how I became a feminist or became aware of feminism and what I started identifying as and why and when and then where it all went and how I became a feminist activist I suppose.

Feminism chose me

Kat Williams

My whole life, I've been angry and in my mind, it has never been entirely clear why I chose feminism. Perhaps it's more the case that feminism chose me.

When I was younger, I was driven by the desire to escape my circumstances, to better my prospects and to fulfil my ambitions. My now-absent father drove us all to the brink of poverty with his alcoholism and debt. Living in this tense, claustrophobic environment for most of my life has undoubtedly left its mark; I have been consumed with guilt for as long as I can remember. I was always the social outcast; the embarrassing truth about my home life hanging over me like a dark cloud. Needless to say, I had few friends.

I believe these initial feelings of unhappiness and dissatisfaction are why I ascribe to feminism; women over the centuries have fought fiercely for even the most basic social mobility and recognition to the fact that they are indeed human beings, worthy of acknowledgement and inclusion. And, I've always liked a good fight.

It's hard to remember how unhappy I used to be; not only mentally navigating the emotional debris that my experiences have left behind, but literally, it almost seems counterproductive to me now to dwell on the past and to obsess over things that I cannot and should not be held responsible for. I think about women who face unimaginable trials in their own lives and who suffer ordeals that we can scarcely imagine and I feel the flames of passion ignite inside of me. I want my life to mean more than my upbringing made me believe was possible.

Women have fought for universal suffrage, the right to get divorced, the right to manage their own finances, access to reproductive health services and still, women and girls all over the world fight for the basic human rights and civil liberties we sometimes take for granted. The constant struggle that women experience in their personal and professional lives to this day is the reason, in my opinion, why feminism is more relevant than ever. We still face the same problems as our sisters before us; sexualisation of women in the media, horrifyingly low rape convictions, renewed threats to our reproductive freedoms, inequality in the workplace, domestic violence...the list, unfortunately, is almost endless.

I am lucky enough to have moved away from home, found my feet and created a new life for myself; some women and girls are not so fortunate. This is why I am a feminist.

Turn your back on Page 3
Francine Hoenderkamp (aged 33)

Was my 'light-bulb moment' at 6 years old when I cut off my Barbie doll's hair into a skinhead and coloured her skin in black? Possibly. The signs were definitely there.

More consciously though, my light came on gradually, happening over a couple of years at around the age of 25 when I started going out with a very old friend of mine from my home town in Essex.

Up until this time I had never really been a socially conscious or political person. The topic of conversation at family get-togethers would always move on to current-affairs, however I rarely had any input; I would be staring out of the window planning on what I was going to wear to whatever party or rave I was heading to that night. I certainly don't recall ever coming across the word 'feminism'.

I moved to London in my early twenties to pursue a career in TV only to return to Essex a few years later to follow my dream of being in a band. It was at this time I moved in with a friend who later turned into my boyfriend. We were of a similar age, from similar backgrounds and with a similar mentality – an 'Essex' mentality to be precise. For those of you who don't know what I mean, Essex is infamously defined by its 'laddish' behaviour and 'Essex Girl' stereotypes. Growing up I was accustomed to its sexist culture - and behaved accordingly - but that was all about to change.

Some of my earliest, uncomfortable memories of my now ex-boyfriend's behaviour was of him being derogatory about the pop star Jennifer Lopez. When Jennifer came on the TV once he made an action as if he was sticking his penis inside of her, with sound effects to match. Similar behaviour would happen if him and his friends got together to scrutinise or salivate over the breasts that were on display on The Sun's Page 3 or in whatever lads' mags they had in their possession. Comments like "look at the jugs on that" and "I'd do it" were all too common.

'Fortunately' for me - for reasons I will explain later – this was just the start of the sexist attitudes I was to find myself surrounded by. My 'ex' once told me that Pamela Anderson had *the* 'perfect' vagina. How would he know this, you wonder? He had seen Pamela's sex tape, of course. *Everybody* had seen Pamela's sex tape. He would, in the future, go on to make scissor actions with his fingers across my labia minora as if signalling that it needed trimming. He would ask me to cut my pubic hair off into a 'landing strip' (instead I grew it into a beautiful, long, thick bush that was to remain there for the duration of our relationship). He would signal that my breasts needed a 'lift' and he also suggested that I go on the pill so as to deepen the sensation of his orgasm when he came inside of me (his orgasm and satisfaction being paramount).

I now know these thoughts and behaviours to be by-products of the pornified society we live in which is conditioning and encouraging men and boys to view and treat women and girls as nothing more than sex objects. Judging them according to pornography's standards and whose sole existence is based upon their 'fuckability'. It is teaching men that women are sexually subservient to them, resulting in a world where our sexuality - physically, mentally and emotionally - is of little importance - if acknowledged at all.

My ex would suggest we watch pornography together when having sex. This usually involved watching two other women (watching 2 men was out the question). I used to oblige, in fact it used to turn me on until I started to wonder why he needed to view other women in pornography to get off. Wasn't I enough for him? Wasn't my body 'sexy' enough for him? All in all pornography didn't leave me feeling very sexy at all.

Other remarks over the time we were together were that my legs weren't toned enough (of course they could never live up to the airbrushed standard that men & boys are accustomed to in pornography and lads' mags), that if we were to be married I would have to take his last name (an archaic and sexist tradition symbolising and marking women as men's property), that he saw nothing wrong in taking his future son to a lap-dancing club when he turned 18 (which is what his own father did for him in order to 'make him a man'). It went on, but it was a combination of all of these examples and their inevitable niggling at my self-esteem and conscience that triggered my next moves. Moves which became the catalyst in changing the path of my life forever. Moves which led me to finding feminism.

Around 2003 (before Facebook!) cyberspace was brimming with feminist bloggers and it was there I found other women with whom I shared similar ideas. Around the same time I also discovered

OBJECT - a grassroots organisation who campaign against the sexual objectification of women and girls in the media and popular culture - and there my journey had started. I can't remember how I initially stumbled across these blogs and OBJECT or what I must've typed in to a search engine to find them, but one thing is certain, had I not I might now be in thousands of pounds worth of debt getting my vagina, breasts and other bodily parts 'corrected'! What I discovered instead was priceless.

I soon started going to meetings and on marches and have done so ever since. I volunteer for various feminist organisations including OBJECT and UK Feminista and have started my own campaign to ban The Sun's Page 3 as not only do I believe the acceptance of pornography into the mainstream as being damaging and limiting for women and girls freedom and progress (my own experiences being evident of this), I also believe the 'iconic' Page 3 to be symbolic of women's inequality in the UK and across the globe.

Feminism has given me a true sense of purpose, of self-worth and self-empowerment. I have made wonderful friends along the way and I can honestly say I have never felt more alive, happy and confident in my whole life. Feminism is my raison d'etre and I will be eternally grateful to my ex-boyfriend for giving me this, for without his unknowing sexism (he too is a victim of our sexist, misogynistic, patriarchal, unequal society) I wouldn't be a feminist activist and campaigning today.

www.turnyourbackonpage3.com

Me and that beauty myth
Hannah Mudge

I don't know if I can say I experienced a 'lightbulb moment' when it comes to my feminism. I tend to see it as being more like a dimmer switch, being turned up, a sort of slowly unfolding awareness of a lot of what was wrong with the world and why it had anything to do with me. It all happened over the space of a couple of years, as I left my teens.

I didn't begin to call myself a feminist until I was about 20 years old. And if I'm honest, I never really thought about feminist issues until I went to university. I suppose this is nothing out of the ordinary for someone like me. I grew up white, middle class and straight in rural England, getting straight As, going to church, playing in the local youth orchestra. None of my friends were even remotely interested in politics or activism. I don't ever remember discussing feminism with anyone, aside from learning about the suffragette movement in A-Level history - and even then, although I felt somewhat affected by it, I never considered gender equality issues as they might affect women in the present day. I think that if you'd asked me, or pushed for an answer, I would have told you that women in the UK had achieved equality - probably because I had no experience of the world, life, or indeed of anything outside the teenage bubble of exams, friendship dramas, hours spent writing angsty journal entries and obsessions with bands.

It was university which was the catalyst. I think that's the case for a lot of feminists I know. Leaving the place you've grown up, encountering different ideas and issues. I started university as an introverted and socially anxious young woman, just turned 19. I struggled with the lifestyle which seemed to go hand in hand with living in halls of residence. To me it felt like just another popularity contest - and those who partied hardest, talked loudest and looked conventionally attractive came out on top. It was during my first few months at university that I started to notice just how much casual misogyny ran rampant. The way I heard some of the guys talk about women. The endless 'contests' at bars and clubs which somehow always seemed to involve getting women to take their clothes off or participate in beauty contests. The pervasive influence of porn and "lads' mags". When I visited my boyfriend, who was studying at a different university, I was shocked by the sexist and degrading content about women in the official student magazine and upset by a string of Playboy-themed events. I was uncomfortable that the conversations of the guys he knew seemed to revolve around assessing the looks and bodies of female students. Everywhere, it seemed that women existed to be objectified and used by men.

I'd always had low self-esteem and during that year it began to consume me. I despised how this culture was starting to make me feel about myself, but no matter how much I tried to remember that I was worth more than what men and those promoting the "beauty myth" thought of me, I couldn't help falling for the lies. I was angry that this culture I was surrounded by seemed to encourage women to do all they could to be everything men wanted; then berate them for being "sluts", criticize them for drinking or blame them if they were assaulted or raped. But at the same time my life was ruled by self-hatred because I wasn't thin enough, or curvy enough, didn't have the right facial features or the right personality or the right clothes to be desirable and important and special. I also found out that a close friend had been raped some years previously. Hearing her story of how she had struggled for years with the impact of what happened, often blaming herself, just intensified my anger and frustration at a system which I saw was terribly wrong.

It was towards the end of the academic year that I started to look for resources online which might help with the way I was feeling - which wasn't good, at all. I tried to avoid human contact most of the time. I'd cry in the changing rooms in shops and vow I was going to lose weight, or get a nose job, or breast implants, or a whole new wardrobe. I sat up late writing raging journal entries about the way I saw women treated, but I didn't know what to do about it. I didn't know my university had a Women's Network - maybe it would have been helpful to me to find people who were interested in the same issues. But as it happened, I started to find websites and blogs. Websites like About-Face, which speaks out against harmful beauty standards and the effects of media and advertising on women. Websites like the anti-porn resource One Angry Girl. This was a time when writing and speaking out against objectification, "lads' mags" and "pornified" culture was starting to appear afresh - and there was a feeling that feminism was making a bit of a return (despite the fact it had never gone away in the first place, of course). I began to read. I found that I wasn't alone. This was, I suppose, what I might call my "light bulb moment". I began to try to talk about it to my friends. If I'm honest, they weren't that interested - but for me, the journey had only just begun.

The next few years involved a lot of education. I was discovering a whole spectrum of topics, all under the banner of feminism. Learning about privilege and all the knotty issues surrounding it. Reading the stories of women from all over the world. Getting immersed in books and blogs and understanding more and more about the issues we face because of our gender. My issues with body image weren't magically cured. It took some years, including through a stint working in the media, when I realized that, contrary to my previous ambition, I never wanted to work for women's magazines.

New issues arose, too. For a couple of years I fought to understand how I could believe in gender equality and be accepted by God and the church - I was attending a church which was conservative on "women's role" and was scared that someone like me didn't have a place there - or anywhere else for that matter. Again it took some time, reading and learning and finding resources which showed me I wasn't alone - but more importantly, that Christianity and gender equality aren't mutually exclusive. In 2011 I've attended two conferences focusing on empowering and equipping women leaders in the church, dealing with theology and the practicalities. While there I met people working to combat domestic violence, mentor young women, challenge negative attitudes among men. I don't think I would have thought this possible a few years ago, because I just wasn't aware that it was happening.

One thing was lacking: community. I still didn't have any "real life" friends who were interested in feminism. The area where I lived had no feminist network or group. Having been subject to a lot of abuse when I'd tried to argue feminist points of view on a forum I frequented, I'd been somewhat put off engaging with new people online, but I knew it was the way forward for me if I wanted to get more involved in activism and talk to other feminists. I attended one of the FEM conferences in Sheffield. I was a steward at the very first Million Women Rise march in 2008. Although I was blown away by the sense of exuberance and community I encountered, I wasn't really confident enough to talk to any of the other women there - something which makes me smile looking back because I'm now the one who's always approaching people at events on the basis that I follow them on Twitter, or read their blog.

These days I go to conferences and marches and meet-ups when it's possible (I don't live in

London; I earn a below average wage. You do what you can and don't feel bad about it). I try to help with organizing things and activism. I started blogging - about feminism, the media, politics and religion - at the end of 2008 and continue to do so because writing's the way I express things. There are issues on my heart which I want to do more about - and we'll see how that pans out. As I get older, experience more and see just how important gender equality is in issues surrounding the workplace, the economy, childrearing, relationships, the law, the press...feminism becomes more ingrained in who I am and who I want to be. I can no longer imagine my life without a commitment to gender equality, knowing the difference it has made to me, to people I know and to those the world over who recognize its importance.

Sisters, mothers, daughters
Maria Margarita Terner

I first became interested in feminism through my sister who was a strong feminist in the 70s.

I saw her fine art degree show and it was a feminist statement on the objectification of women's bodies.

Later I joined a women's group at university.

The pivotal moment for me was reading Susan Brownmillers "Against Our Will'.

This book shocked me and affected me deeply. I felt such outrage and anger as a consequence that

I felt motivated to become active. I joined the London Rape Crisis Centre which was run by feminists where I made some amazing friendships and found solidarity and development of my ideas about myself as a woman. I also met a lot of lesbian feminists and widened the scope of my awareness of women. I got involved in several campaigns such as WAVAW.

I have not been active since the 80s but I am interested in current feminist ideas, particularly gender issues. I feel these are pivotal to current awareness of sexual politics.

I still like to stay in touch with feminist ideas and have the convenience of having 2 daughters who are involved in very different ways.

I love to see them grow as women with their own sense of who they are in this society. I feel that maybe I have had something to do with their openness to feminism and that satisfies me.

Questioning gender roles
Rose Clark

My Mum and Dad were feminist activists in the 1980s and I later grew up mostly with my Mum and sister. As a teenager in the 90s, I didn't get feminism. My Mum would get bothered by sexist adverts on the TV and me and my sister would groan, 'we KNOW Mum, just let us watch the programme!'. Now I know how she might have felt, but it just didn't seem important at the time.

I really came to feminism myself partly through the awareness that my parents had and also through being differently gendered, i.e. never wanting to fit into neat categories of femininity and masculinity. If you don't feel comfortable in the gender roles that you are expected to fulfill, I think you naturally question the roles themselves, and are already on the road to feminist modes of thought. I eventually came across queer feminisms that dealt with questions about my own gender identity, and picked up on the second wave feminisms that my parents had been into, but emphasised the whole binary gender system as a source of problems. That's where I'm at now. I'm not sure there's been one moment where I suddenly realised that the feminist arguments were important and had great weight. I have moments like that all the time, but also lots of moments of doubt and confusion. 'Feminism' is a word I'm comfortable with using, but is so multiple in its meanings, I'm still finding out what it means to me.

One reason why I'm a feminist: a confession
John

Let me first say this: My firm belief in the importance of feminism stems from my firm belief in the importance of equality in all its forms. My belief is that the things we perceive to separate us, be they gender, ethnicity, faith, sexuality, financial status or societal role are the result of a conditional illness; they are merely a symptom of the neurological disorder which comes about through the delusion of our individual importance, and result in only pain and oppression. I hesitate to explain the root of this belief, as I suspect I will never be able to analyse it completely in a way which will satisfy or convince the reader, or even myself, but I shall try to take you through what I understand to be the progression of events and experiences which led to this conclusion.

Allow me to begin with a cliché; I had an unhappy and confused childhood, which led to an unhappy and confused adolescence and later to an adulthood marred with deep, clinical depression. The reasons for this are many, but I would like to suggest that the initial cause for my difficulties stem primarily from the existence of a gender divide. I am by no means a martyr nor a masochist, but I feel my journey towards my identity of a feminist is an interesting and unique one.

My recognition of gender division and distorted body image began at a painfully early age, through no fault or effort of my own. Being born six weeks prematurely with a slight malformation of the legs, feet and genitalia resulted in many serious operations and years spent in casts and figure realignment. Had I been born in a less developed country, I would never have been able to walk.

Whilst I count myself deeply lucky for the fact that I can indeed walk, I spent my early childhood without the full use of my legs, in almost constant pain of some sort or another. I was unable to join in with typically 'male' past-times, most sports throughout my childhood, teenage years and indeed today remain inaccessible to me for any length of time. I was also continually told that I would be unable in the future to partake in those other prescribed boyhood fantasies; the idea of becoming a military serviceman, a fireman, a policeman. Indeed, every two months, my visits to the hospital came with a list of jobs I would never supposedly be able to work in (although, interesting, on that list was 'lecturer', which is my current position). I cannot help but feel this was significant also in the creation of my perhaps unusual later identity.

My development into what is perceived as 'male' was undoubtedly effected by this exclusion of boyish things, and resulted in my exploration of typically female childhood hobbies – I was enthused by knitting, and began my lifelong obsession with literature, nature and the arts during the times when my peers were chasing balls, jumping and running. I was unconsciously setting myself up as something 'other' through what I perceived to be the options available to me. Indeed, this went further still, my submergence in the world of all things feminine (also a result of living in a household where I was the only male) seeded a fascination into what seemed a world of secrets – I was preoccupied with cross-dressing, and my life, it seemed, would be simpler, less painful and humiliating, were I not of my gender.

Indeed, I was frequently chastised by all for my 'feminine' attributes – I was, and remain, a deeply sensitive and emotional person, particularly prone to crying. I was often told by teachers and parents to 'toughen up/man up' – words which I still flinch at.

It is an uncomfortable truth that the ideas of what is sexually desireable or appropriate for the opposite sex are formed and reinforced at an extremely young age, and both sexes were seemingly in agreement that physical prowess was a desireable attribute for the male to possess, something which was out of my reach. I was also unfortunate enough to be heavily scarred by three operations up the entire of the back of my legs and along each foot – I remember clearly being told by girls at the age of six that the sight of me in shorts made them 'feel sick'. We may consider such young children to be innocent to the world of physical attraction and revulsion, but this is clearly a myth.

Television, Hollywood, parents – all things exist as agents of socialisation priming children for the illusion of success in a competitive society. People such as myself, who were by default forced to reject that which is desirable to the opposite sex fall by the wayside. I look back on this period as a time when I had the beginnings of a choice-which-was-not-a-choice; I could feebly attempt to be 'a man', as my male peers would tirelessly and enthusiastically spend each minute doing, or, I could embrace 'the other'.

This, I chose.

I threw myself into a world of art and music and books, and galloped through my teenage years with the same confusion I had always felt, but expressing it as strongly and as visually as I could. I began wearing makeup, growing and dying my hair, proclaiming my femininity as loudly as I could and revelling in gender-bending confusion, attracting verbal and physical abuse – my own form of self harm which distracted from my genuine depression and confusion which wasn't realised until years later.

To question gender roles in puberty and adolescence was, for most, unthinkable. Here is a time when sexuality and sexual identity is at its most confused, yet most fervent and righteous. My upbringing and childhood experiences had not allowed for any declaration or display of masculinity, and my teenage years were the emerging (and at times tasteless and brazen) results of this. Neither male nor female peers were happy – this is obvious. The girls were pressured, agonising over their physicality, the boys were terrified of the rate and result of their changes, all were emerging from the chrysalis of childhood with immense fear about how they would end up once the metamorphosis was complete.

I was not apart from this, but understood it in a different way. My shame and fear came about in perhaps more unusual ways - I was literally ashamed of the adult man I was slowly becoming. With little male influence in my life, and my childhood desire to escape masculinity (indeed, I had always harboured the idea that men were somehow imperfect, unkind, unwelcome), I kept the natural changes in my puberty as secret as possible. The gender divide was becoming obvious, and I genuinely was embarrassed and ashamed of this. Where most adolescent boys celebrate the day they begin shaving and have the support of their male family members in guiding them through dragging razor blades across their face, I began shaving in secret, hiding safety razors under my bed as if they were something taboo, and mopping up blood from my lips as I literally didn't know what I was doing. People must have noticed, and I wonder why it was never discussed, why assistance was never offered. The shame in my transition was unshareable, and the feeling of disappointment, of letting down my female-dominated family life was real and actualised.

Alongside this, I suffered for years in silence between the ages of thirteen and seventeen of an intense and intensely painful swelling of my testicles. I assumed that this was normal, that it was part of the same process which was deepening my voice and sprouting hair on my body (something I still to this day have deep discomfort with) and ignored it until finally visiting a doctor (again, in secret) and being told that it was a collection of fluid which had resulted from my premature birth. I found out at this time that I had a large scar on my scrotum from an operation I never knew that I had. My genitals, my maleness and male body had never been discussed with me.

I spent a long time deeply bitter about these facts – it felt to me that the gender divide which was such a prevalent subject in my life had in some way endangered me, and began to realise that whilst this type of discomfort and confusion may be (or indeed may not be) unusual amongst young men, it was almost typical of young women resulting in a plethora of problems regarding the perception of their bodies against an unattainable or non-existent ideal. I continue to live what many would consider a 'feminised' life with 'feminised' problems – my enthusiasm for poetry and art, for flowers and fashion has developed alongside my obsession with my appearance, my constant fears and anxiety about my weight and distorted image of my body.

And so, you may be asking how this is entirely relevant to my status as a feminist and gender equalicist. I believe the answer lies in the fact that I see and saw the divide, the statuses and roles we fulfill in society being reinforced by every agent of socialisation in subtle, insidious ways from the earliest ages. We are offered choice, but to choose anything other than the gaudy dichotomy of pink or blue, of dancing shoes or pick-up truck has serious societal consequences which would and have crushed people into submission or over-compensation for generations.

The belief that we are divided, separate and disconnected could be seen as the sole result of misery, oppression and violence. My story is not one of deep, unassailable suffering, but I continue to live with mental problems and side affects which I believe stem from the separation of male and female. It would possibly be tempting to make a judgement about my sexuality from my words about my childhood preoccupations with cross-dressing and make-up, but this leads me onto the idea of fluidity. The idea that there is not even a *third* choice, but the removal of any choice from pre-orchestrated options which only serve to benefit a dichotic capitalist system of this, or that. I refuse to assign myself a sexuality, but this is simple, as it is something hidden, something interior. Should I choose or had chosen to refuse a gender, this would be impossible, perverse. And thus, I label myself a feminist for the primary reason that I refuse to accept judgement by gender, reinforcement of gender, death or suffering or pride by gender.

Finding a wider recognition of equality
Jessica Metherington-Owlett

There was no single moment when I suddenly realised I was a feminist. Rather, I had a series of slow realisations. I was brought up in a middle-class, liberal household, and my parents installed in me the belief that all individuals were fundamentally equal and should have the same opportunities.

As a child, I countered some boys' assertion that "boys are better than girls" by saying that girls and boys were the same. As a twelve or thirteen-year-old (and an early developer) I physically fought boys who made unwelcome comments about my body, and because by that point I had the strength of an adult, I always won. To the extent that I thought about comments, I assumed that boys who said derogatory things about girls were doing it to tease. It didn't occur to me that there could be people who genuinely thought men and women were unequal.

My teenage feminist stirrings can be drawn to an incident which happened when I was 18. I was in two car crashes in the space of a month, both of which resulted in my car being written off. The first was a case of someone else damaging my car, the second an unusual situation when I skidded on ice changing lanes on a dual carriageway and only a more experienced driver stood a chance of regaining control of the car. The reaction of my male friends – jokingly, but more than once – was to suggest that I must be an awful driver. Yet when a friend wiped out half his tail lights doing handbrake turns in a multi-story car-park, there was no suggestion that he had been a bad driver.

My second click moment was in fact a series of moments starting when I went to university. I grew up near Brighton, and had assumed that all universities were much like that. Imagine my surprise, turning up properly suited (leather trenchcoat) and booted (DMs) in Durham to find that it didn't look like a university town at all. To be honest, I was too shocked at the lack of goths to notice the lack of feminism.

That's not to say that Durham was particularly sexist. However, it was at Durham that I realised how deep the divisions between political stances really go, and had the first opportunity to uncover my own political views. Some of my friends discovered they were socialists and collectivists, others that they were libertarians and individualists. Other people were, I'm sure, too polite for their sexist views to be obvious. A housemate of mine revealed herself to be more than simply personally insecure when her brother visited – whereas before she seemed shy and modest, in his presence she suddenly appeared positively submissive. The same housemate found herself amazingly embarrassed by bodily functions if a man was in the house. I assumed that these were childish affectations which she would grow out of.

I had a similar series of clicks in my first job. After University I worked for a Conservative Member of Parliament and found myself alongside some immensely privileged young women, and it came with a shock to realise that they didn't have to fight to be heard – that our society is still so elitist and so divided by class that these privileged women had never considered that they could be perceived as unequal to men. And in my experience, they were treated more respectfully than less privileged women; everyone listens to the posh lady wearing a pashmina.

I had expected to find Parliament testosterone-filled, rage-fuelled and deeply sexist. But I didn't. I found the institutions themselves to be individualistic, neutral, finely balanced between tradition and logic. It was working in Parliament which led me to explore the fluid meaning of "masculine" and "feminine", and the differences between politics and society. While I found some of the parliamentary procedures to be inefficient, I never considered politics to be masculine. Certainly there was a clear hierarchy, but what I saw was based on age rather than gender, with researchers of all parties brushed aside as frivolous, if academically brilliant, young things. We were all in our early twenties, too ambitious to stay for more than a couple of years and so issues of child care, so often the stumbling block to women's careers, simply didn't arise.

The conflicts between my libertarian heart and feminist head have shaped my political beliefs and led me to liberal feminism. I am an individualist rather than a collectivist, believing in individual choice unfettered by legislation or social expectations. I cannot support a notion of a platonic ideal, an "essence" which can be defined as "woman". How can women, who make up more than 50% of the population, truly be a united group, truly have the same interests? I'm not certain I believe in men and women, just in people.

I don't just believe that men and women are equal, I believe they are fundamentally the same. Of course there are statistical differences – we are, after all, talking about two groups of 30 million people in the UK alone. And of course the society we live in leaves an indelible mark. But fundamentally, I believe that a girl, plucked at random from the UK population, has as great a natural propensity to numeracy or creativity or anything else as a boy of the same age selected equally randomly. I find it sad that children are so often encouraged to behave in a particular way, leading many to ignore their natural talents.

I think the future of feminism lies not in a politics comprised of narrowly drawn legislation, but in social attitudes and a wider recognition of equality. Speak up for equality, stand up for equality, fight for equality, but don't think that it's obtainable simply by making a law.

In defence of ideas, or, how I became an angry, self-righteous, man-hating bitch
Ray Filar

When I was a young kid I didn't have many friends, mostly because I couldn't reconcile the amazing world I saw in stories with the shitty, boring world I lived in. Social skills were something that I acquired belatedly, if I can be said to have them now. At primary school, reading books was the height in uncool. I stole a copy of *Thames Doesn't Rhyme With James* off the cupboard in my classroom - it would have been too much to openly take a book home. Shaking in excited fear, I spirited it away in my bag. It wasn't very good.

One friendless summer I spent seven hours a day trawling through a fantasy series; a level of concentrated dedication I have tried in vain to recapture since. I would read until I was busting to wee and my eyes and head ached and I was starving. Then *Harry Potter* happened, and reading was slightly more acceptable. But the fictional existence of brainy Hermione was not quite enough to rehabilitate me in the eyes of my peers. She was an early feminist heroine of mine, but one heroine, let's face it, ain't enough.

Things haven't changed much now I'm a bit older. I've read a lot more, and I've discovered that other people exist who think it is ok for women to be more interested in ideas than in winning the approval of others. I was afflicted from an early age by feminism, but it took a long time before I put a name to what was wrong with me. Even now, being a feminist is challenging, difficult and isolating. It means breaking silences, objecting once, twice, and then again, again, again. Objecting forever. Sometimes, it's deliberately killing the fun. It's saying 'I don't find that funny' when everyone else is rolling around on the floor. It's constant questioning, becoming, endlessly travelling away from what society calls womanhood. Trying to be a feminist can, and will, make you a crushing bore to those people who aren't. You may as well make yourself a giant 'broken record' costume and cement your quivering body into it right now. Sister, you just chose the hard way.

Six or so years since I began to self-define as feminist, I can hear patriarchal oppression calling seductively. Look at those sexy shoes (the shoes whisper). Isn't it nice to have a strong man's arms around you, to take the weight, as Toni Morrison would say, off your breasts? So wasn't feminism about the right to choose? For every woman who 'chooses' the sexy shoes and strong man's arms I know there'll be a gender essentialist wanker proclaiming the death of feminism. Who needs nuanced critique when there are headlines to write? I want to know why almost all societies eroticise garments that restrict women's freedom of movement. I want to know how sexy high heels are different from sexy bound feet. How about considering that maybe women desire support because we have so little economic and political power of our own? How about we start with the right to choose; then maybe let's look at how, and why, we make choices.

As a child my mother internalised within me many useful maxims, which today sit in my head to be vocalised, in my mothers' voice, at the most inopportune of moments. *'There is no such thing as boys' toys and girls' toys'*. I'm sure I repeated this ad infinitum in the playground at about the same time that the pretty girls in my class formed the 'I love Scott' club (Scott didn't give a damn; he was having fun playing football with the boys). At about the same time I also decided to tell kids that Santa didn't exist, a golden truth which nevertheless did not win me the reams of admiring followers I had envisaged. Later on I watched in confusion as bright girls acted stupid.

They pretended they didn't know the answers. I got the message and stopped trying at school as my classmates giggled, flirted, and tossed their long, straight, glossy, well-groomed hair. Without knowing why we were doing it, we began to fall in line with the centuries of socialisation which dictate that women should be seen, if attractive, but never heard.

I became quiet, unsure of myself, and then I became rebellious. I was excruciatingly aware of the awkwardness of my presence. When I walked through the school gates in the mornings, I knew that my black Kickers were clunky and unfashionable compared to the sleek pumps of the girls whose mocking eyes followed me as I went past. I was frightened to walk alone, or speak audibly, or take up space. These are the bonds of femininity that gender fascism creates. I can't remember my mother's exact maxim from that time, but we talked a little about the pain of womanhood. In my pre-adolescent mind womanhood equals pain. Period pain, waxing pain, plucking pain. The pain of being fucked. The pain of constant sexual harassment. The greatest pain, for me, was the pain of beginning to understand my designated social role. We inflict womanhood on our little girls, then we tell them to deal with it. At this point I started listening to Marilyn Manson, wearing black makeup, and smoking dope in my room.

And anyway, my mum wasn't completely right. There *are* such things as boys' toys and girls' toys, in the same silly shallow way that there are such things as boys and girls. Because we have dictated it shall be so, so it is. And my hair will always be frizzy, my profile will always be Jewish, I will never look as well groomed as those who can more easily approximate Barbie, and since I came out as a feminist I will (try to) always state, nay, shout, my fucking opinion as loudly as you can shout yours.

During the Manson years I started to think, vaguely, cloudily, that there was something wrong about the sexual double standard. That the sexual shame heaped upon the girls at school who dared to have sexualities, or (gasp!) who let media appear documenting their sexualities, was destructive and unfair. I wanted the school to do something about it. I wanted girls to talk about the fact that it wasn't just boys who masturbated. I wanted a discussion about why sex was structured around the male orgasm. I wanted to know if the female orgasm existed, and if it did, why I wasn't having them. I wanted to know if wanting to fuck women made me a pervert, or worse, a lesbian. I wanted sex education that acknowledged my existence.

So I started to read some different books. I read Ariel Levy's *Female Chauvinist Pigs*, then *The Female Eunuch*, *The Second Sex*. At university, I read

Backlash, Woman Hating, Gender Trouble. These books, each of them, were life changing moments for me. Every time I read a new feminist or queer book or blog or write a blog of my own, I am stunned by the power of their contents. Their ideas allow fuller formation of the partially examined dissent that floats around in the back of the head. If you don't read, you're stuck, I'm afraid, with half-formed dissent.

Quite obviously, I love talking about feminism. But if I have to have another discussion with a progressive, liberal white dude who wants me to scientifically prove how all-pervasive objectification and endless representation of women as passive, hairless fucktoys has *maybe, just maybe,* got something to do with rape and sexual violence, I will scream. Please don't make me explain again that there is a Back. Lash. against the perceived advances of women's lib - that yes, I KNOW that there was rape before internet pornography, that this doesn't make a difference to the point. If I have to argue, again, that women generally don't lie about rape because women generally aren't liars - I will give up on human interaction and retreat to the feminist section in the library for evermore.

Except I won't. I'll carry on having that discussion again, and again, and again, because that is part what it means to me to be a feminist. If I can convince one of you to pick up a copy of *Toward A Feminist Theory of the State*, in my mind I've changed the world a little bit. When I go on, and on, and on about the same shit, the same status-quo defying arguments which should really be a matter of sheer common sense right now, it is because I don't understand why you don't already think this stuff. But if every so often I give up and just shout 'READ SOME FUCKING BOOKS WHY DON'T YOU?!', please let me off the hook. It's boring and repetitive to be a feminist.

I will always remember the poster on my English GCSE teacher's wall. It carried the legend, 'well behaved women rarely make history'. It's ubiquitous, but that was the first time I saw it. I remember a conversation that took place in my girls-only class, 'Miss, why do we have to read so many books written by women?' My teacher, an acerbic New Zealander, replied, '*because I'm bored of reading books written by men.*'

Anyway, at some point, there it was. Feminism. It slid under the door and into my wholeheartmindbody. Maybe it didn't click right then in English lit lessons, or during the time of not being able to talk to boyfriends, who mostly failed to notice or act on the fact that my mid-sex 'ow' noises were not earth-shattering moans of pleasure. It wasn't when I wanted to go out and live my life but was dissuaded, as I might get raped. It wasn't when I made first eye contact with a lesbian on a train and felt the force of it reverberate from my toes up to my eyebrows. And it wasn't at exactly the point that I read *Female Chauvinist Pigs* and realised that I was one. But by the time I got to sixth form and I was taking place in a Facebook fight (I know, I can't let these things go) in response to groups, set up by boys at my school, with titles like: 'The Masculinists - a celebration of traditional values', 'Boys are funnier than girls', etc, - I was a feminist. Back then I was still at pains to assure people that being a feminist didn't make you a hairy lesbian, which now seems rather ironic, but even so, I was a feminist.

As I grow up, I can, more and more, see my own misogyny. Feminism is a class movement first and foremost, but it's also an individual's struggle to be better. It is difficult to be constantly alert to giving women's words equal weight with men's, to making sure that I don't prioritise men in conversations. I try to notice every time a woman is interrupted whilst speaking, and not do it myself. I make sure to read books by women and listen to music made by women. In the face of what we are taught, I try to trust women, to love my female friends, to not automatically dislike women I feel threatened by. But you can't shed misogyny just like Jennifer Aniston sheds boyfriends (oh no she di'int!). It's internalised, it's cultural, and I am just one angsty, irate and perpetually disappointed member of a relatively small movement that sets itself at odds with the very systematic foundations of society.

I once heard Bonnie Greer argue that feminism was about enabling a full humanity for everyone. I took her to mean, in part, that feminism is a holistic philosophy of hierarchies, a full outlook on power relations. I'm pretty sure that bell hooks said something similar some time before that. This is the closest that anyone has come to fully explicating what it means to me to be a feminist. Class analysis and race analysis may be separate philosophies too, but at the same time they are integral to feminism. It is about women of all colours and all classes embracing subjectivity - about claiming right to our own personhoods, our own narratives, and our own desires. That's what feminism is to me. Being a feminist doesn't make me happy all the time. Mostly it makes me angry, sad, disgusted and just overwhelmed at the sheer cliff face of the task ahead. Being a feminist means increasingly I can see just how far we have to go before we have anything remotely approaching freedom from the oppression of gender.

From "fair" to "just": a tale of two feminisms

Marina Strinkovsky

As far as I can tell, I've become a feminist twice. So far.

The first time, I don't really remember the exact moment, but it was definitely a long time ago, when I was really quite young. I noticed at an early age that calling myself any kind of "ist" made people jolly cross, which seemed like a good result to me; and I've been a cheerful socialist atheist feminist pacifist environmentalist ever since! It is not unlikely that my dad flung the word "feminist" at me in the middle of a row – "what are you, some kind of feminist?" - that sort of thing. Chances are, a combination of pluck and contrariness made me adopt the label there and then.

In any case, I was born with a highly developed sense of fairness, and a very clear understanding of my own worth. It was never going to be much of a leap from that to a primitive conception of social justice: it's not fair that people are poor; it's not fair that women earn less money; it's not fair that all the politicians are men; it's not fair that we have war; it's not fair. Especially as applied to, well, me.

There were other, more specific influences; I clearly remember, aged 13 or 14, reading the recently published Handmaiden's Tale, and my instinctive reaction was to double cross my legs and think:

"nononogetawayfrommyuterusaaghnowaychoicechoicechoice!"

You know. In that way you would if you'd just seen Aliens for the first time and realised that could actually happen to you. Anyway, so that took care of the pro-choice part of things, which was just as well really, because in most other ways my feminism, from the age of about 12 to 35, consisted of not much more than sassing authority figures and doing everything I thought would be widely considered rebellious and controversial. And annoy my dad.[see endnote 1]

The list of political accomplishments from this era isn't terribly impressive: I played around. I dropped out of university. I married someone I wasn't supposed to, and kept my name. I refused to do ironing (actually, that's more of a feminist act than you'd think - not the ironing, the refusing – but more on that later). I smoked and drank and cursed and was scrumptiously unladylike. I espoused radical politics. I was, in short, a complete and utter victim of the 90s: a third wave wannabe in thrall to a worldview that said feminism was a pair of fishnets and a bad attitude. [see endnote 2]

Then something quite unspecial and commonplace happened to upset the apple cart: I left my husband. Because I was fed the fuck up with a man who, on top of his other major character flaws, was always wearing crumpled clothing. And that gave me the opportunity to do, read, think, say and try a lot of things that were not easily possible to me in my marriage. I don't mean to say that I'd been controlled or limited in my marriage; it's just that when you live with someone, you try and accommodate their tastes and preferences. You try not to cook food they hate, play music they loathe, or be active in politics they don't agree with.

Armed with an appetite to do all the things I'd not done while married, I launched myself into reading about feminism: everything from the I Blame the Patriarchy blog to Simone de Beauvoir.

And here's a funny thing: I realised I didn't actually know jack shit about feminism. Isn't that funny? I mean, how many of us go through life calling ourselves feminists, when our idea of feminism is the exact same media driven caricature that the anti-feminists use to bash feminism? Mindfuck.

And then...The kind of off-planet parallax that you get when you suddenly see the world from the point of view of people you'd never really understood before. Here's a thing: things don't look the same from over there as they do from over here. When I was picking off young men to have my wicked way with, they were "passing" me from hand to hand. When I was speaking up in class with opinions that I thought were as clever and correct as anyone's, they were indulging me like some sort of performing monkey (at best – at worst they shouted me down). They – men -

simply hadn't gotten this memo I seemed to have been reading from, where I'm, like, totally a fully fledged human being with all the same mental capacity and sexual agency as them, you know? And, infuriatingly, there ain't a damn thing I can do about it – because there's this thing, I realised, a thing bigger than I am, that screws up the way I and everybody else sees the world, and it's called Patriarchy.

I'd sort of spent my childhood and youth operating on the assumption that with enough brio I could simply break down any barriers of sexism that came in my way, topple them with sheer awesomeness. Now I began to know that patriarchy had happened to me. Husband's crumply refusal to do any housework? Patriarchy. That promotion I'm stubbornly not getting? Patriarchy. Street harassment? Patriarchy, baby. That time in high school when I was struggling with maths, and my teachers encouraged me to drop the subject rather than bully me into success? Yeah. Boys and young men who disrespected and bullied me? Brought up in a patriarchy, they didn't know how to approach someone who so obviously didn't understand their allotted role in life. [see endnote 3]

Another humbling mindfuck was how futile, on this view, it had all been: my rebellion, sass and refusal to conform were a tiny part of why the world kept pushing back on me; frankly irrelevant compared to my instinctive and utter failure to perform my gender properly. I could have been tattooed from head to toe or bristling with piercings and living in a commune: as long as I did the ironing, had babies, and didn't insist on talking in mixed company as if I really – shockingly! – truly believed my opinions mattered, and – even more horrific! – fully expected to be listened to and respected, it all might have been OK.

By simply believing that I was as smart and as worthy of notice as anyone else, I was being this uber-scary undermining agent of the radical matriarchy [see endnote 4], and I wasn't even trying! Because until I actually started to read up on feminism, I just didn't see the strings of gender attached to my arms, didn't realise that all my frantic pulling was against those strings and not against some more visible external forces like fairness and whether or not it was my job to make sure the toilet got scrubbed.

But hey, you can't change the patriarchy at the level of the individual; that is one of the more painful things I realised on this journey into feminist theory. You can be awesome and oppressed by it.

I dunno, maybe it's a good thing that people should realise that in their thirties, and not have all the wind knocked out of them by the awful truth when they're still young and full of beans. But in hindsight it's blindingly obvious that however ground-breaking and successful one remarkable person manages to be, however many individual, single Madonnas or Amelia Earharts or Marie Curies we have, the superstructure won't budge – you have to change the world for all women, or you've changed it for none. Which is kind of exhausting and demoralising to even just think about, but there you have it.

I'm not saying that things like fair pay and toilet scrubbing aren't important; they are. As is representation of women in government, media representations of girls and women, access to education, the sex industry, violence against women, and rape conviction rates and and and…But to concentrate on those things in isolation, to try to solve them as discrete problems, is to miss the point: patriarchy is not in the details. It's the whole thing. It's the water we swim in, which is why we so often fail to notice it.

To get rid of patriarchy, we need to undermine its basic tenet: that women are not full humans, but lesser beings open to special treatment, and that they need to know their place and police it themselves. We need to move from conceptions of fairness in specific situations – from being individually awesome, all on our lonesomes, one by one - to a fuller understanding of what justice for human beings as fully realised moral agents truly means. And that's the new and improved kind of feminist that I became when I became a feminist for the second time: the kind who wants to just do away with the whole rotten goddamned system and put something better in its place. No, you know, pressure or anything.

[1] That's actually not really true. I was always terrified of my father and craved his approval, like every normal little girl, but it was clear early on that his approval was not forthcoming. I thought that was because I was flawed and unlovable, but now I think it was because I was a little girl who didn't know her place, you know? But it's easier to make jokes about I guess.

[2] Don't judge me y'all! Camille Paglia was, like, a bona fide public intellectual back then, OK? I had bad influences! I was young and impressionable!

[3] I'm not saying that I'm so likeable that every man who's ever been mean to me has done it Because of Patriarchy(tm). But it's certainly true that challenging people's expectations is not a move that ensures you popularity, so when you go through life deliberately flipping off social norms, you get the occasional "fuck you, bitch!" in response.

[4] There may be an operational tip there for future revolutionaries.

Finding a feminist community
Rose Child

For me, like a lot of others I expect, there was no single instant when I suddenly realised I was a feminist. It was more like a steady 'drip, drip' at the edge of my awareness, as I came into contact with feminist theory through my studies and, afterwards, encountered the gender divides in the 'real world' of work. I'd never described myself as a feminist during my teenage years – I'd never even been into "girl power" during the Spice Girls craze of my schooldays. I'd always believed in equality between the sexes and, since learning about them at secondary school, had always held a great admiration for the suffragettes and what they'd done for women in the UK. But to me that wasn't feminism, it was just common sense. Surely that was what everyone thought?

My eventual move towards feminism was a selfish thing, I guess. As a child and young adult, I'd never really felt disadvantaged by my gender, so what did feminism have to do with me? I grew up in an all-girl household with the exception of my father, and had always been able to hold my own against the boys at school – it was mostly the other girls that ripped me to shreds. But once I reached a certain age – sexual maturity, I suppose – and moved away from the sheltering environment of home, sexism started being directed at me in a more obvious way, and suddenly I began to care a little bit more. Not quite enough to label myself a feminist though.

But over the next few years, and particularly during my postgraduate year at university, I studied a large amount of feminist theory and literature as part of my degree. There was no single part of it that made me think "Yes, I'm a feminist" - in fact, I disagreed with a lot of it. But at the back of my mind something must have struck home, and I gradually began to see how many of these ideas were still relevant in modern society and how they applied to me and my life. And, finally, I came to the realisation that the views I held *were* feminist views, and always had been.

That, I suppose, was my light bulb moment, although it was largely subconscious and stretched over a period of months. I attended my first discussion group with Bristol Feminist Network, and I've never looked back. At first I jumped in feet first, claiming any view that called itself feminism as my own and vehemently defending them to all and sundry. As they say with religion, there is no-one as fervent as a convert. Gradually, however, I began to temper my views and even now I am still working out what I really think about certain issues. I began to realise that I didn't have to get involved with and have an opinion on every little thing; I could be a feminist and support the cause in my own way, using my own skills.

I also initially fell prey one of the biggest misunderstandings that there is about feminism: the idea that all feminists agree on every so-called 'feminist' issue. This seems to be a view held not just by non-feminists but by a lot of feminists as well, and it's certainly what I assumed when I threw myself into the movement. It came as an unsettling surprise when I found myself strongly disagreeing with other feminists about particular issues. But if these differences of opinion ever get me down, I remember that we have the same end held strongly in our minds – equality – even if we have different means of getting there.

Now, my prevailing principle above any of my political or ethical affiliations is common sense. I try to ignore the propaganda and try never to ignore the facts, no matter how opposed to my views they are. I have no problem changing my stance on an issue if a good enough case is presented. I want my views to remain fluid, and avoid becoming set in my ways; I never want to think I have all the answers. I feel like I'm growing into my feminist views, and growing up at the same time. I know that my views are no less deeply held for being on the more moderate side. Despite any amount of uncertainty regarding specific issues within feminism, I have no doubt that I am a feminist, that I will remain a feminist and that, above all, I am proud to call myself a feminist.

Finding my sisters
Siân Norris

Considering it was my idea to put together this anthology telling the moment we became feminists, I have found it extremely difficult to discover and tell my own. Was it, as I often joke, the influence of watching Maid Marian and Her Merry Men on TV as a child, with its outspoken female lead who ruled the roost of men? Was it when I was 16, and my friend Nadia lent me The Whole Woman, a book I devoured and then parroted for years, until as I got older I began to question some of the things in my feminist bible (notably the transphobia and her comments on female genital mutilation). Was it my feminist teachers at school and university who encouraged me to write essays on Djuna Barnes, Katherine Mansfield and Jean Rhys whilst everyone else was doing Joyce and Milton. Was it my early activism in the anti-homophobia movement and the influence of having two mums, a dad and a stepmum?

It was, of course, all these things. As well as organising Ladyfest Bristol 2007, writing a feminist zine and blog and ultimately co-ordinating a feminist network of a few hundred women and men.

But the more I thought about it, the more I put my actual, lived and activist feminism down to a period in my life of depression; and the decision I took to stop it, to move forward and to be happy. And I think a big part of this for me was in learning about and discovering sisterhood.

In the anthology that inspired this book, Click, one of the writers says that feminism was her consolation prize for surviving an eating disorder. I feel the same way, except that my form of self destructive behaviour wasn't around food, but self harm. Self harm is lonely. It is about struggling to deal with emotional pain, so turning that pain on to yourself to try and control it with a physical pain. I cut my arms and legs with shaving razors from the ages of 16 to 20, with a few gaps in between. I don't know now if I could really articulate what the emotional pain was, if I even understand now what it was. But I know that it was real and it was big, even though now I can't really name it. And the only way to make it manageable, to make it small, was to turn it into a physical pain.

During one of these bouts of depression I wrote the following story. I can still remember the anguish and the anger that fled out of my pen and into the A5 ringbound notebook on my lap, in that freezing cold room I lived in in Dalston (this was 2005 guys, before the hipsters moved in). I wrote it after having been sexually assaulted on a bus by a man who leaned over and grabbed me and tried to kiss me:

"The bus is making me feel sick. Everyone is playing a game of musical chairs that they haven't told me about. Every time it jolts to a stop, everyone seems to get up to swap seats, and I'm just left sitting here. The man behind me is talking about the weather.
This is the most awful bus journey. It is worse than the one with the woman talking to me about her boyfriend who used to beat her up, or the one where the man tried to kiss me and I had to push him away hard.
It jolts again to a stop and it is my turn to leave the game. I walk fast down the street, it's dark,

and each time my foot hits the pavement I jump
that it is someone else's. My whole life I have been
afraid of the no one behind me on the street.
My key sticks in the lock, but I battle it open. The
living room is crowded with lived in mess. There's
drinking, but I go to bed instead.

My body slides down, sinking into the valleyed
mattress. The covers are heavy, but I'm not warm.
I daydream about a mattress that I don't sink into.
That doesn't collapse along with me. My room
isn't dark, but it's peaceful. The water pipes
gurgling remind me of my childhood. Being afraid
of the witch that lived in the boiler cupboard.
Next door, I can hear my housemate having sex.
She has thoughtfully turned the music up, but all it
does is emphasise the fact that there is another
noise to cover.
The mattress is swallowing me. My back is melting
into it in a sticky mess and I can't unglue myself.
My legs have stopped working. I grab the top of
my left thigh to see if it is still there. I think maybe
it is. I imagine my hand is yours. Whichever one
of you.
My fingernails are dirty.
It's disgusting. I know I should clean them, but
you can pretend they're not.

Sometimes, when it starts to go this way, when it
gets to feeling that my bones collapse; I can feel
every filament in my body. I can feel my brain

moving against my skull, it is creaking, and when I move my eyes, I can sense the scraping of them against the sockets. I feel it in my neck. I can see every little pore in my lungs open up. I can track the blood rushing to all the drought-ridden places in my body, I can hear it squealing. I can feel the cells' pain when they split and break and crack into two parts. I can feel a tension under my breastplate every time my heart remembers to try and convulse.

It makes me wonder what my body looks like to an outsider. How it feels to the hands that grab it and to the tongues that smear it. What it is in my body that inspires such strength in another, that triggers that burst of love and steals that loss of control, and what it is in my body that defies all that, so the hands scuttle away like little crabs.

Slut body.

Sick body.

My body.

It belongs to all of you.

It isn't that no one cares. It is that no one cares enough. And the hands that grab and touch, and the lips that grab and touch, push me away and I fall back on the mattress that swallows me up.

Gulp.

Lying in bed, my body shrinks to the size of a pin. My legs retract and my head and my arms are pulled in and I lie there, a pin. I'll prick your prick your prick pricks me.

But it's changing. Now my body crumples in on itself, and I crinkle and crack and all that's left is a piece of dirty newspaper, with two hands kneading it, and I can see my mouth in its folds. Or is it more than two?
The hands pull the paper flat, and suddenly I'm white and clean and smooth and plain. I lie there still and blank, and you can write me, as you will.

You draw me a face of the wide eyes of your ex, while You and You put on the big lips of the girl you're in love with, and of course there's You who paints on the cute smiling cheeks of the girl that You are in love with still, whilst You let me keep my nose, to remind you that it is me you're using, but You lengthen my hair and give it a new shade to suit a generic fantasy. Then I'm ready for all of you. And I lie here for you all, I'm hidden, I'm curled under my flat stomach and I love you all and I love you all and I think yes this is it this is it this time surely one of you will stay. But then you collapse on my breasts and then you rumple my hair fondly and then you stand up. My eyes behind her wide eyes are blinded. You lift the white sheet with its attractive additions and go back to who they really belonged to all along. You leave me my nose and my flat stomach.

Anytime you want me to, I can make you happy. There's nothing I won't do, just to make you happy.

And you all know it.
And you all know it.

So you can leave me with the safe knowledge that I won't.
So you can go back to the real wide eyes and the real big lips and the real cute cheeks and the original better, bigger, brighter mix of parts, and know that you can always come back. Lay a clean sheet over the crushed blood and bone on my dark dark dirty sheets and re-draw me to make you happy.

It's good to be here.
It's some kind of bliss.

But you know and I know that my bed isn't enough. You are all frightened to admit it, but I know that you all know. So although I lie here in wait, it is no surprise to me when you don't come back.
I lie here in wait for the next time you need attention and flattery.
And for you, I lie in wait for the next time you argue with her and need some comfort.
Whilst you know I lie in wait for you for when you want to feel good about yourself and your power over me.

The longer I wait, the more changes you all need to make to the paper. Soon you must close your eyes when you come; to make sure you don't catch sight of my real face behind what you paint over it and I fake it oh and I fake it ah and I fake it don't stop and I fake it that's right and I fake it harder and I fake it faster and I fake it yes!

Anytime you want me to, I can make you happy. There's nothing I won't do, just to make you happy."

I decided to use this piece of writing to tell my story because writing it was my light bulb moment. I think that despite having always called myself a feminist, despite reading Greer and writing academic essays on gender and mouthing off about all sorts of feminist subjects; despite all of this I hadn't been acting like a feminist. I had been careless with myself and I had been careless of other women. I had let patriarchy in through the cracks of my book-ish armour and not only had the result left me unhappy and struggling; it had also left me silent on the subjects of how men were treating the women around me, as well as how they were treating me.

Years later, when I thought about this period of my life, I remembered a man I had slept with laughing about how he had pulled this woman, had sex with her and then left because he realised how 'ugly' she was. At the time I remember thinking this was awful, but not challenging it.

After I wrote that story, I realised that I couldn't call myself a feminist if I continued to refuse to treat myself with respect and failed to treat other women with respect. So, a few months later, I stopped self harming. I stopped sleeping with people that I didn't want to sleep with. I stopped reading celeb magazines and joining in their mocking of other women's bodies. I stopped judging what other women were wearing, or saying or doing. I started to treat the women around me as sisters. I realised that I wasn't going to like every woman I met, but that wasn't what sisterhood meant. Sisterhood, in a feminist sense, meant seeing a commonality with women, and a commonality in the way patriarchy harms us.

This didn't happen over night of course. It was a process of years more consciousness-raising. But it started then.

Some say that the concept of sisterhood is an outdated one. But I disagree. Sisterhood was my saviour. Now, many years later, I am surrounded by sisters in the feminist movement. Of course I owe my change in confidence and happiness to lots of other things too, including counselling, friends, family, boyfriend. But my feminism, my strength in my sense of sisterhood and community – that's what started the change. I saw that I had to wake up to how women were being treated, and how I was complicit in patriarchy's project. And that feminism and sisterhood could make my world a better place. So, slowly, I started working within this feminist sisterhood to ensure that the pressures of patriarchy that hurt me would not be around to hurt my one-day daughters.

Now that I am a fully-fledged feminist activist, sisterhood is even more important to me. As I learn more about global inequality and how patriarchy impacts on women and men in so many destructive ways, the need to reach out to women across the world has become vital. The fight against patriarchy isn't just about fighting the ways in which it hurt me. Being part of this global community, this global network, gives me the strength and enthusiasm to keep going, to keep fighting. Together, a better world is possible.

Inspiring others to their light bulb moment
Lucy Jones

April 2004: I'm in my first proper job after university, working as a sales manager. Though young, I have been successfully managing a small team of telesales staff and sales representatives since December. I meet two new clients this month. The first begins to send inappropriate text messages to my work phone after meeting me only twice, and repeatedly asks me to go out for drinks with him. He's in his thirties, married with children. I'm 21. The second is an older man whose eyes tend to rest about 10 inches south of my face when talking to me. He discovers that I am to be responsible for the sales operation for his product. As I begin to explain the strategy that I have developed, he interrupts me: "Well, we'll have to get a bloke in here to help you – we can't expect a pretty little girl like you to manage this all on your own".

These incidents make me feel angry, cheapened and unfairly discriminated against because of my age and my sex. I tell my friends about these men, who I describe as 'sexist pigs', and we all agree that it's outrageous that – in this day and age! – people would behave like that towards a young woman in the workplace. Yet was this my light bulb moment, when I discovered that I was a feminist? No.

October 2004: I've given up on sales after feeling constantly belittled, and have decided to return to university to see what I might make of myself in academia. I'm now 22, and I'm sat in a pub with my new colleagues on a Masters course in linguistics. We're talking about ourselves, our interests, what we hope to get out of our postgraduate careers. I tell them that I'm a lesbian and that I live with my partner. I'm asked outright by a left-wing, well-educated guy who is a bit older than me "so, presumably you're a feminist?" A fair question, but one I take offence to. Just because I'm a lesbian, you're assuming that I'm a feminist?! My answer? "Err no, I'm not a feminist! I don't burn my bra!"

April 2005: I'm sat in the university library, reading for my dissertation for the same degree. A dissertation which has taken me down the path of understanding cultural perceptions of gay and lesbian people and, unsurprisingly, has led me to several key feminist texts. I begin to read about feminism and queer theory, and become intrigued – this phenomenon which I'd always thought of as extremist, man-hating, 1970s hippy nonsense actually begins to make a bit of sense to me.

The more I discover about the history of the Women's Movement, the more I start to understand not only why it began in the first place, but that the battles have not all been won. All of a sudden, while sat surrounded by books in this library, the incidents in my sales job come back to me. So, too, do the countless times that I have been made to feel stupid, inferior or vulnerable over the years, the moments that bothered me at the time but which I'd put down to individuals being 'old-fashioned' or 'sleazy'. The boys at nightclubs who, when I'd turned them down and explained I was a lesbian, opened their flies to show me the "good cock" that I "just needed inside" me. The older men who had wolf-whistled and beeped their car horns as my friends and I walked down the road aged fifteen, leaving us unsure of whether to feel scared or sexy. The peer pressure to wear tiny skirts and to apply makeup which would, as the teen magazines I'd read when I was younger described it, 'draw attention to the mouth and make boys think of what you might do with it'.

These moments suddenly come together as evidence of a patriarchal culture with a current of misogyny running through its core. Every incident that had ever made me feel uncomfortable because of my sex, I realise at this moment, was a consequence of the culture in which I had grown up: one where it is okay to position women and girls as sexual objects, where lesbians are perceived as malfunctioning women who need a man to straighten them out and where women are viewed as less capable than men in the workplace. I instantly remember my comment months earlier about burning my bra, and my cheeks burn. I realise that feminism might mean something to me after all – something beyond the stereotypes and superficial jokes surrounding 'women's lib', something which is collective and which demonstrates that the way that women are typically viewed in this society is damaging. Once I actually understand what 'feminism' means, I realise that it has been a part of me all along, and I regret the years that I didn't recognise it. This is my light bulb moment.

Now: I am a lecturer at a university and teach a course to which feminism is absolutely central. In the first lecture each time the course runs, I stand up and tell my students this story. I tell them that they don't have to be feminists to pass the course, but that they have to understand it. Somehow, the label still terrifies young women and men and is enough to make them shut down and stop taking in the messages that matter – like me, when I thought it was just about burning your bra. I find myself gently coaxing them towards feminism, for fear of scaring them off all together. We spend time on the course talking about the cultural expectations of women and men, and I encourage them to think about their own experiences.

Usually, by the end of the course, most people in the class have found themselves agreeing with some kind of feminist statement, principle or idea, and even expressing feminist arguments themselves. Yet most of them will not identify as feminists, largely because they fear that the label will make them stand out as some kind of freak.

Sometimes, though, those that do view themselves as feminists after this course will come and tell me so. I feel proud to have been able to trigger their own light bulb moment, but sad that it took until now for them to have it.

Because we should all be feminists
Matt McCormack-Evans

I have often been guarded about discussing my motivations for becoming a feminist activist. My suspicion is that many of those who have asked were seeking to make sense of me, to explain me away somehow. To the question 'why are you a feminist?' I usually respond, 'because it's right. Because everyone should be a feminist.' That rarely satisfies though. 'Is your mother a feminist?' or 'do you have sisters?' are common prompts that follow.

It's hard to say how much my family contributed to my becoming a feminist. Whilst my mother is a strong woman, she's never identified herself as a feminist, and although I have three younger sisters, I feel what's perhaps more important is that I was aware, from a very young age, of the abusive behaviour, both past and on-going, of my maternal and paternal grandfathers. Hearing from my mother and grandmother about the physical, psychological, and economic abuses carried out by those men left strong impressions on me that strikingly conflicted with the equality I saw in my parents' relationship.

Beyond this family background, my becoming a feminist occurred gradually. There were, however, several 'light bulb moments' along the way. The first of these took place when I was around 16. I had a very close relationship with my girlfriend at the time, and I believe that when you are in such a close and empathetic relationship, you can occasionally get glimpses of what life is like for your partner, a bit of what the world looks like for them. Through this relationship I felt I saw snippets of how differently the world treats women as a group.

One thing that came across strongly was how differently our culture expected us to express our sexuality. While I was enveloped into a mainstream hip-hop and 'lad' culture that celebrated an aggressive masculinity that was relentlessly contemptuous of women, my girlfriend and female friends were learning that their sexuality was something to perform for men and that more than almost anything else, our culture valued them for their appearance. It was then that I sought out and became a regular reader of the feminist online magazine, The F-word.

However, in spite of this early introduction to feminist thought, at university I stopped reading The F-word, and on a background of living and socialising with a group of young men I slipped into what I suppose was a pretty typical male university student experience. I also started using pornography more than I had ever done previously. My first contact with porn took place at around the age of 11 or 12 in the form of porn magazines, hidden in corners of playgrounds and parks or under friends' mattresses. I bought so-called 'lads' mags', like FHM, on a regular basis and then progressed onto internet porn at around age 15 or 16. This all occurred without the influence of an older brother or father who used porn. At university, with my own computer and room, using pornography became a regular part of my life.

Despite this, I still challenged my male peers on some of their sexist attitudes; on buying *The Sun* (with its page three), on going to lap-dancing clubs, on their 'protecting' women, etc. I also had a strong reluctance to study anything feminist or gender-related. This was not because I wasn't interested, but rather because I wanted my studies to be an academic abstraction from the real or practical world. I knew I cared too much to treat feminism in a dispassionate unemotional way, which was proven to me through an inappropriately heated discussion in a Jurisprudence seminar on Dworkin and MacKinnon.

It was around this time that another significant or 'light bulb' moment happened. One night I noticed the cut lip of a female friend. I asked about it and the answer I received didn't seem quite right. I asked again later, and what followed was the start of a friendship like no other that I have ever had or ever will have again. Over the subsequent months I learnt that my friend was the recipient of physical, psychological and sexual abuse that took place within her home, and had done since her early childhood. She didn't fit the stereotypes that I had learnt of someone living with abuse; no one would ever guess what she was going home to. I was hit by the realisation that it didn't matter what people looked like or did, almost anyone you see in the street or know in your life could be living with all kinds of violence and abuse. It angered me that this kind of violence, violence against women, is so silent and is so often closer and more frequent than many of us know.

At the same time, perhaps partly as a result of being confronted by the knowledge of violence that was happening to someone I cared for so much, I challenged the excuses I had used about my use of pornography. I began to see more clearly, or perhaps just stopped lying to myself, about the sexism, violence, and degradation of women in mainstream pornography. My questioning of pornography continued through the writing of my undergraduate thesis about racial embodiment and the power of cultural representations of racialised individuals and groups. This took me to the feminist authors bell hooks, Audre Lorde, and Simone de Beauvoir. It didn't take much to recognise the very similar processes at work in colonial propaganda's and mainstream hip-hop's influence on how black people are racialised and perceived, and how pornography informs the cultural understanding and conceptualisation of women and girls.

I had told myself that I could partition my porn use away from my attitudes towards women, but it became increasingly obvious that this was not possible. I also became aware of how pervasive porn use was among my male friends and grew more receptive to events that revealed the influence that pornography had on how they saw and thought about women. One example was the questioning of whether a female friend's sore throat was because of deep-throating rather than a cold; another when some of the men my then girlfriend was living with - after giving one of their number 'birthday beats' - suggested to another woman they were living with that they give her 20 'cum shots' in the face on her birthday. I was angry about how porn was informing the attitudes of young men in such an unchallenged and insidious way.

My thoughts on the representation of women and girls in our culture became more definite and upon completion of my thesis I immediately joined the feminist organisation OBJECT. A few months later I was doing voluntary work for them, and soon took up the role of Membership Officer for the group.

After leaving OBJECT to return to education, I set up The Anti Porn Men Project. The Project is an online forum for (mainly) men to speak, discuss, and learn about porn, porn culture and the anti-porn movement. There was no easy-to-find space online to hear from men who objected to porn. I wanted to create such a space, where those who were developing anti-porn thoughts for the first time could read material that would legitimise their concerns and help them feel like part of a wider community and movement. The Anti Porn Men Project was launched in September 2010 and received over 10,000 visits in its first 3 weeks and media interest spanning 6 continents in the following 2 months.

Moving forward, I want to develop workshops for schools and sixth-form colleges, pursue greater support for the anti-porn movement in both feminist and left-leaning political circles, and to keep pushing for it to be more socially acceptable for a man to be vocally feminist.

It started with a manifesto
Jenny Rintoul

This 'manifesto' marks the point at which I recognised myself as a feminist activist. What began as an academic interest in feminism in my early 20s, developed in to a drive to take action that has not quelled since writing this manifesto in 2006. At that time a work colleague said to me: 'usually this interest in feminism is a phase you go through when you are younger, I wonder why you haven't grown out of it and are still in to it now?'. By the following morning the manifesto was written and a copy was on each of my colleagues' desks...

I consider myself a feminist concerned with gender issues in visual culture. I am 27. I am not unhappy with, nor disinterested in, my own appearance. I am not anti-men. I am not a prude. I am not pro-censorship.

My concern is the normalisation of sexism.

I am anti the normalisation of sexist pornographic imagery (that which objectifies women and assumes a heterosexual male audience). This 'normalisation' takes place in one way through 'lads mags' which:

a) depict females in pornographic poses that fit a very narrow and specific model of female sexuality (one that supports – and constructs – the stereotyped heterosexual male fantasy), and yet are displayed alongside all other magazines in newsagents and supermarkets, and

b) contain material (articles, photos) based on the one-dimensional view of female sexuality mentioned above, yet which purport to be a view of 'normal women' and their sexuality (all models are depicted as, and all articles are based on, 'the girl next door', and thus these magazines are about attainable and 'normal' women). With competitions like 'Win your girlfriend a boob job', and free gifts like life-size cut-outs of a large-breasted, slim nude female torso with instructions to 'position this against your girlfriend', the message of sexism in these magazines is rendered 'normal' and applicable to all women, not just 'porn stars'. And who receives these messages? Boys, men (and often their girlfriends, especially with competitions like 'girlfriend of the week' – pose in your underwear like the girls in this magazine and the photo with the most page-three potential gets printed), not hardened(!) porn-fans.

Lads mags are not localised in sex shops. They do not have an '18' certificate. They are read by:

a) young 'lads' with little sexual experience whose views on female sexuality are built through material like this (it is not exclusively 'lads mags' that support a sexist view of women; music videos and other forms of popular culture also conform to sexist stereotyping, all confirming that the one-dimensionality of female sexuality *must be* inherent to women!).

b) readers' sisters, girlfriends, female friends, who view themselves in relation to not only the celebrity women to which they are regularly exposed, but more realistically to the 'normal' women that are sexually exploited in 'lads mags'.

The reason that this is so potentially damaging is that it is *cool* (and packaged as 'empowering') to be the victim of the heterosexual male gaze. For a start, Playboy merchandise is sold to children as 'cool'; when that child discovers what Playboy actually stands for, she will also have to confront what she has been supporting. If she backs out now, she is rejecting what is fashionable and 'cool', and so desirable, plus she is rejecting the identity that she has been tricked into forming for herself. But she does not need to back out, because it is not just the Playboy bunny that this young girl can aspire to be; 'lads mags' come to the rescue. 'Lads mags' give her a far more attainable target; those women in Nuts and Zoo are 'girls next door' just like she is.

c) adult 'lads' whose views on sex and women have been constructed through this stereotyped material.

I am anti the lack of choice in widely accessible pornographic material. The heterosexual male is largely favoured as the intended audience; if the heterosexual female chooses to engage with this material, she does so under the guise of the male heterosexual gaze. With the display of material like 'lads mags', that 'choice' is extinguished (as these images are unavoidable if you ever venture onto a high street), and thus this narrow and restrictive model of female (and male) sexuality is depicted as a given, with no consideration for ACTUAL sexual orientation (i.e. the existence of homosexual women is denied, there is room only for the 'lipstick lesbian'; females, irrespective of sexual orientation, are available for male consumption).

Perhaps by definition pornography cannot be egalitarian as it is rooted in submission and control. There is certainly scope for a type of erotica that empowers both (or all) parties involved, but as long as 'lads mags' retain their identities as 'normal magazines' depicting 'normal women', sold in 'normal shops', the constructed definition of female sexuality as a one-dimensional response to heterosexual male desires, remains.

So…Go into your local newsagent/supermarket and take action: cover the lads mags with the magazines displayed nearby (children's magazines are usually in easy reach); move the lads mags to the top shelf; gather the lads mags and hide them under a display cabinet. Alternatively, ask the manager to move this material. Trading standards did advise in March 2006 that these magazines should be 'out of the sight of children', and you're therefore able to reprimand offending outlets. If the manager is not willing to comply with your request, ask for his/her name and contact trading standards.

If I were to write a manifesto now, in 2012, it would not look like this. If I were to update or edit this, it would read differently. However, I present it here as I wrote it in 2006, to mark that point when I started to become involved with feminist activism. Incidentally, my identity as a feminist has not wavered; feminism is at the heart of my value system, and I don't think I'll ever 'grow out of it'.

Get on the bus
Maureen Beck, Just Women magazine

Am I a feminist? Until quite recently I would probably have answered *No* to this question but now my answer is *Yes*. I think I have always been a feminist without knowing it, hence my involvement with causes related to improving the quality of women's lives in our society.

I believe the Women's Movement has improved the life of women, but further improvement is necessary. We need women with feminist ideals to get in there and do something about it.

I am sure that some people think that feminists are anti-men. This is not necessarily so. Wanting equal rights, opportunities and choices for women does not mean being anti-men.

If our society was adapted to women's biology I believe both sexes would be much happier. If children's needs were included when assessing the needs of women we would be halfway there. Have you ever seen a young mother with toddler, baby and pushchair in tow trying to get on a bus? If men had to do this every day I am sure buses would be adapted very quickly.

Women should choose where they give birth, and who their carers are, and have the opportunity of household help after childbirth. Childcare facilities should be available to all mothers, enabling them to have some time for themselves.

I believe maternity rights should be extended, and discrimination against mothers in the workplace be ended. Why isn't compassionate leave allowed when children are sick? For that matter, why shouldn't allowances be made for a difficult menopause?

Am I looking for an ideal world? I don't think so. I would just like to see a world fit for women to live in.

Summer 1992

Working together to switch on the light
Jan Martin

I don't have a light bulb moment as such, more like a gradual turning up of the dimmer switch. A friend told me I was a feminist when I was in my mid twenties (over half my life ago) but I didn't believe her, and it took a few years for me to realise that's what I was.

Several years after that I started working at Cardiff Women's Centre, running the second-hand clothes shop. It was then I began to realise that my, until then, unformed thoughts were actually feminist thoughts, and I began to make sense of my experiences in a feminist context. I looked back at my formative years and realised that pretty much all the problems I had experienced as a young woman could be traced back to male/female inequality.

I had body issues – I was slightly 'overweight', and aware of how undesirable that is. So I was lacking in confidence.

I had health issues – caused by the pill, which (mostly male) doctors prescribed, but then didn't know how to fix, and didn't much care.

I had emotional issues – caused by experience of sexual and relationship violence/abuse; this was coupled with total confusion within relationships: with pressure to be sexually active from a very young age, and the contradictions I saw in the 'we-must-have-sex-but-if-we-do-you're-slag-and-I-won't-like-you' approach to physical intimacy, which allowed men a guilt-free sex life but not me.

I'd always had a stifling feeling of injustice and of something not being right with these double standards. But everyone else acted as if this was normal, and I felt odd, so I blamed myself and my own bad luck for the particular set of problems I had to deal with. Feminism began to light up these confused spaces.

But my real light bulb moment – i.e. light fully on – has only happened in the last couple of years, since working with Bristol feminists, and at the same time finally working through some of the issues that had dogged my life. What I realised was this:

There are no physical, moral, intellectual, emotional, spiritual, political or cultural standards which haven't been set by a male-dominated value system. There is no refuge from sexism – whether it is in politics, art, work, religion or interpersonal relationships. There is wisdom and truth, on occasions, in all these areas, but genuine wisdom and truth is hard to spot amongst the age old 'wisdoms' we've been fed so long and that have always been instrumental in keeping women in check. Our ideas about the 'good' ways to behave, think, feel, write, create, speak etc. are all set by the patriarchal system which gives greater validity to men's voices. These ideas are distorted because our world order is distorted by that system.

I am much less likely to find solace in art, literature, music; or in gentle philosophies of forgiveness and love; or in personal 'self-development'; or the thought of romance, or career success, or any of the other ways we find comfort that allows us to acquiesce in our own oppression. In fact I think maybe we've been looking too hard for solace and comfort. All of these ways of processing our anger and negative experiences have been framed by patriarchy. It chooses everything for me: from the books I read to the news I hear; from the clothes I wear to the fundamental spiritual/moral lessons I've always been taught, and what constitutes a 'good' person. There has never been any other context in which to explore such stuff. Trying to express yourself outside of the framework is to invite censure, or be ignored.

I feel deeply ambivalent about all 'standards of excellence' now. And always when reading, listening, watching, learning I try to take out the filter of authority which tells me 'this is beautiful' or 'this is profound' or 'this is accomplished' or 'this is just'. For the self-validation of the patriarchy is ubiquitous and persuasive – and must always be challenged at its root.

Once you have seen through this filter the light comes on full, and it's pretty harsh. But working with other women has made me grateful for the clarity. You can't switch it off again anyway; all you can do is keep speaking your truth as you see it in these moments of clarity. Hopefully, if enough of us do it long enough, eventually the old hegemonies will shift and standards and values will come to encompass women's perspectives.

Then maybe we can begin to change the patriarchal distortions which have led to the catalogue of injustice, corruption, exploitation, and misery which constitutes our current world order

We will no longer accept that 'men will always rape', or 'true equality is impossible', or 'people are inherently selfish', 'men are inherently violent', 'life is suffering', 'there'll always be wars', 'the poor will always be with us', and all those other potted wisdoms that uphold our world as the only possible one, and which patriarchy needs in order justify itself. Then maybe relationships will be equal, divisions between male/female work and pay will disappear; pornography will die out; men will take their share of caring for the young, old and sick (in fact their share of all work); sexual and gendered violence will stop; women will have peace, safety, and autonomy in all walks of life; and their thoughts and experiences will have universal validity.

Keep on saying it.

The dust was off the doormat forever
Peggy Walker, Just Women magazine

I came to feminism quite late, my early life being happy but conventional. It offered no feminist role models. At first I thought poverty was women's oppression but grew to realise it was only one aspect. I always resented sexist behaviour and sexual harassment, but it was not until my two daughters were teenagers and already feminists that I seriously considered sexist language.

We had many discussions over coffee and freshly baked cakes after school. I've always felt they added a great deal to my education. One day they told me I was a doormat, citing the cakes as an example, even though they were enjoying them. I was horrified. They pointed out the hours I spent in the kitchen every day and said they'd like me to be doing something for myself instead. At that time I made all our bread, cakes and preserves. I was told "If this lovely food is all you want to do in life, then fine, but there are so many other things you are interested in…"

On reflection I realised they were right, and as I thought of my own and other women's situations, I wanted change. Eventually I developed a life outside the home with political activities of all sorts as the focus. From being a wife, mother and armchair socialist, I became an activist on many fronts. Life became exciting. Once I spent fourteen consecutive weekends away at Greenham Common, conferences and demonstrations. I learned avidly. Now instead of cooking an evening meal at no set time, but when my husband was ready for it, I was off to happenings on the other side of town. The dust was off the doormat forever.

To me feminism means striving for social and legal equality with men and to change the traditional role and image of women. To eliminate sexism and to appreciate the experiences and qualities unique to women of all ages.

Summer, 1992

Woman, mother, feminist
Helen Mott

When I was a postgraduate student of social psychology in the 1990s, I remember attending a conference presentation where members of the audience were asked to think about their social identity. We were asked individually to write down three words describing our social identity. I can't remember what I wrote then, but reflecting on it now, I know that I would choose *woman*, *mother* and *feminist*. These seem to me at this time in my life to be the core 'lenses' which shape both how I am perceived in the world, and how I act in the world.

I was not always a card-carrying feminist. While feminism was not itself in the vocabulary of my childhood, I was brought up to value social justice, equality and fairness – and I can't think how anyone can hold those values without being a feminist – it's simply a question of whether the 'label' applies. I was brought up in the Catholic faith too, which of course carries and promotes strong messages about sex difference and (biological) determinism. The idea behind the name of this book's imprint – Crooked Rib – was significant in my life and I used to love the quote:

> *Woman was created from the rib of man,*
> *She was not made from his head to top him;*
> *Nor of his feet, to be trampled upon by him;*
> *But out of his side, to be equal to him;*
> *Under his arm, to be protected by him;*
> *And very near his heart, to be loved by him.*

I don't think I ever really believed in God, but I did used to believe in this benevolent heterosexist stuff about gender roles. I must have thought it was romantic.

Growing up in the 70s there was nothing like the pressure there is today on children to be branded by gender in everything they do and wear – the 'pink princess' brand wasn't around, everyone was in browns and oranges as I recall. It was much easier to just be a child. Then I went to secondary school and was one of a very small number of girls in what had been, for a couple of hundred years, a boys' school. On the one hand, academically there was no differentiation at all – we learned woodwork and technical drawing but not home economics (excellent, as far as I was concerned). And there was no concept of gender playing a part in subject choices. But on the other hand, alongside this pedagogical gender-blindness, girls were required to be differentiated from boys by their uniform – we could wear open-neck shirts while the boys wore ties (why?) and we were not allowed to wear trousers but had to wear skirts (why?). Then as time went by we observed the school creating new subjects for the girls to do, like the vile netball. And they introduced an after-school cookery club. I found this confusing and annoying.

When I was 16 I left home and school because I couldn't wait to grow up. I lived in a bedsit and worked in various sales & office jobs. That year I went on holiday to Cornwall with a group of friends. At that stage in my life I hadn't really been exposed to hostile sexism. Most of my school friends were boys. I didn't have many female friends except for my 'best friend' who was, like me, untroubled by the social requirements of femininity. Growing up, I don't think we had ever been expected to play with dolls, help with housework (although it was only our stay-at-home mothers who ever did any housework) or place any value on the way we looked. As teenagers we behaved just as the boys in our peer group did: I suppose we were 'ladettes' before the phrase was invented. However, I was gradually becoming increasingly aware of the sexual double standard – hearing the ways that young women would be talked about and judged by their male and female peers. I was also beginning to become aware that some of my young women friends were troubled by their weight, or body shape, and would put considerable effort into restricting their diets and exercising obsessively. I didn't like to see that. Anyway, before going on that holiday I plundered my parents' bookcase for something to read. The book I picked up was The Women's Room by Marilyn French.

It's been years since I've read that book but the memory of that first reading is still with me now. The unfairness! The heartache! The sense of going with the narrator on her journey of understanding. The narrator's world was close enough to the world that I had grown up in to resonate on a personal level, at least in terms of the questioning about traditional gender roles and the exclusion of western white, educated, middle class women (like me!) from intellectual life, careers and full personhood. So, that was the first illumination and the seeds of my identity as a feminist were sown. I absorbed the ideas in the book but didn't really do any more than that. I didn't know anything about feminism as a movement and I wasn't driven to seek out books or conversations about feminist ideas, basically because I didn't know anyone who had feminism on their radar. But my mind was opened to questioning the validity of the gendered status quo.

A couple of years later, I went back to college to study for 'A'-levels and picked Psychology. I fell in love with psychology, specifically social psychology which I went on to take a degree in later. I have a vivid flashbulb memory of sitting in Psychology class, watching the tutor chalk up on the blackboard "Kitty Genovese, NYC, 1964". The story of Kitty Genovese's fate has been referred to as a modern parable in psychology. She was sexually assaulted and murdered by her attacker outdoors in New York in a number of separate attacks which were reported to have taken place in view or hearing of no less than 38 witnesses: we learned that nobody intervened or called the police until after she was dead.

This was my light bulb moment.

The parable of Kitty Genovese has so many layers that it still attracts attention from psychologists today. Some of the most shocking claims made about the number of witnesses, how much they witnessed and so on are now disputed. But on one level the facts are simple. A woman was sexually attacked and murdered by a man, and her suffering and death were preventable. She died because male violence against women was seen as private business, because her life was not valued enough, and because not one witness overcame their social inhibitions in time to help her.

This salutary story and other adventures in social psychology (learning about bystander apathy, conformity, obedience, prejudice, self-delusion, in-group and out-group behaviour, 'imagined communities' of interest, social identity theory…) turned me into an activist as well as a feminist. I learned to have a healthy suspicion of ever doing something just because 'everybody else' is doing it – and a healthy suspicion also of *not* doing something just because 'nobody else' is doing it. I learned that the power of social conditioning is an enormous force to be reckoned with. I also learned that by opening our eyes to the social forces at play in maintaining the oppression of women, we can weaken those forces and overcome them.

Accused of being a feminist!
Clio Bellenis

I didn't so much become a feminist, as discover I'd always been one. I was on holiday with my cousins (who are Greek/Italian) and whilst there, they accused me of being a *feminista*. This was early 1974, I was 16. I had never heard the word before but it was clearly an insult. On getting back to England I checked to see if there was an English translation, and was a bit shocked it had been used as an insult as it seemed to be a description of common sense. I became instantly proud to use the term and have been an active feminist ever since.

There were small things going right back that I was careful about and didn't understand - at 6 years old I learned to tell people that English was my favourite subject because I got fed up with the reaction when I said Arithmetic. I used to get the same difficult reaction at the age of 9 (1966) if I said I might like to be a doctor; another girl in my class who said she wanted to be a nurse got a much better reaction - yet we were both equally able. I knew I didn't want my mother's life (although she was happy with it) but it wasn't until after I self-consciously assumed the appellation 'feminist' that I realised I didn't have to forsake having a family in order to have a career as well - I didn't think it was fair, men seemed to be allowed both. At the time people were seen as 'career girls', or had families. I knew when I was still at school that no man would ever support me - maybe that's just control-freaky but it was very wise. I think being at an all-girls secondary school protected me from quite a lot of sexism growing up.

I'm now nearly 53, I married for love rather than security, then divorced but earned more than him so I bought him out; gave him half of everything we owned, and was able to separate without financial wrangling. I am still an ardent feminist and wept at the silly concept of 'post-feminism', as if we have yet even achieved equal pay for equal work. I watch young women with children having to give up their jobs because they have an ill child and are not allowed to use annual leave for emergencies. I could go on: the use of language, personal presentation, dual standards in the law never mind anywhere else, but I won't bore you with stuff you probably already know.

One final point, as a junior doctor in the early 1980s we had group which Susie Orbach facilitated for the first year of its life, it was shortly after they had set up the women's therapy centre. Not sure how that's relevant, but it was part of a journey (as they say).

For the record my mother (born in 1933) was not allowed to go to university as they 'weren't having a bluestocking in the family'. She never resented this and has always both been happy with her life, and happy with my choices too.

Crowing about trauma: becoming and staying a feminist
Debi Withers

I became a feminist because I wanted to be part of a social movement. I wanted to be part of a groaning, unrelenting machine of protest, creativity and resistance that led to permanent and unquestionable change. I wanted a feminism that was anti-racist, anti-capitalist, trans and queer positive, which embraced the non-human as a vital political force, challenged ableism of all kinds (visible/invisible), was trans-generational, without borders and able to practically think through a new world imagining, bookish but militant, creative and cunning, compassionate. Revolutionary.

During sleepless, fearful nights in the late 1990s when I think I first 'became' a feminist, I contemplated the social and political landscape I inhabited, clutching my copy of Plath's *Collected Poems*, crying heavily into my pillow. I was so alone. There was no movement to participate in where I could positively release the anger and lack of belonging I felt. Teenage angst, yes, but it was serious. I was a sensitive young queer woman with gender issues, a rape survivor with quickly deteriorating mental health. I was hurt. Feminism, I thought, was my answer, and it did help. It gave me space to dream, to yearn, to know that the world that abused me was not the only reality. I could break free, I could heal, but it took time, and, in fact, with every day I move in this world, I realise I am *still* recovering.

I did, eventually, find my movement. One mental breakdown and several books later, I finally crawled into flesh and blood (pre-Facebook!) social networks where, amidst dirty squats and collectively prepared, cheap vegan food, I would find my political kin, at least for a time. I liked it and it felt like home. Not alone!

But radical feminist and queer communities are difficult places to be in. There is the euphoria of finding like minds – initially, that sense of unity – but then the inevitable cracks show up.

There is all that trauma flying around too.

I really wish that feminists would take more care with each other. Learn to relate in a care-full way. To avoid the temptations of internet 'dialogue' which can be so destructive. Be aware that people are often trying their best (with limited resources) and that they will make mistakes.

People who are engaged with feminist activism in an in-depth way are often survivors of abuse and painful situations. In this society I think most women experience a continuum of violation. Some women are physically violated, while others may feel the day-to-day tolls of psychic abuse that are prevalent just about everywhere, and in all of us. If your experience is impacted by racism, homophobia, transphobia, ableism and so on, this will add a further twist to the tale. Likewise, some women will also experience privileges of race, class and sexuality that make their journey through the world a little easier. It makes it easier for them to speak and occupy space that other women have little hope of accessing. And that is totally fucked up and needs to change.

By saying that we are survivors, abused, I don't mean to say we are all victims. I think there is often a knee-jerk reaction to talking about the pain women can experience in order to not seem weak, in order to present the image of unassailable strength. Of course I think it's important to show that survival is possible and a reality, but I don't want to do that at the expense of acknowledging vulnerability, or noting how abusive experiences impact on how people relate to each other, how they communicate and sustain relationships in the long term.

If we look over the course of feminist history, and popular interpretations of it, you can detect cycles of inevitability. These are doom-laden stories that keep us stuck in ruts of permanence. One of these is that feminists will always fall out with each other – the reason why feminism 'fails'. I don't ascribe to this because change is *always* possible, cycles can always be broken. Having participated in feminist and queer social movements, I can see, however, why such a story is repeated. It has a lot to do with the elephant in the room – trauma – that shapes a lot of political interactions.

There needs to be so much more respect, care and awareness of the gradations of trauma that accumulate when a mass of women, queers and sometimes men, get together to organize collectively around feminist issues. If we don't put that kind of awareness in place we will always turn against each other is painful and destructive ways. In all my time organizing collectively, I don't think this issue was accommodated into understandings of the work we were doing. And that has consequences.

I am still interested in being part of a feminist movement that is able to work through difficult problems using care, dialogue and creativity.

Although listening to the crow singing, most days, seems more appealing.

My story
Natalie Collins

Before I start I would like to say I am a Christian. I love God with all my heart and since I began learning His truth that men and women are truly equal I have worked with everything that I am to challenge the Powers which keep patriarchy in place and stop equality being realised.

A decade ago I began a relationship with a severely abusive man (let's call him Alan), he put me down, made me feel worthless, useless and alone. He raped and degraded me, made me hate myself and isolated me from almost every friend and family member. He destroyed everything I had ever been.

I thought he did this because of his bad childhood, because he was depressed and agoraphobic. I thought he hurt me because he couldn't help it and because I made him the way he was. It was my fault really. Apart from the fact he had abused every female he had ever had a relationship with, it couldn't have been their fault too…could it?

Then he assaulted me when I was 6 months pregnant and my son was born 3 months premature. My 2 year old daughter and I lived in hospital with him for 5 months until he was able well enough to leave hospital.

It was my son's birth that turned my life around; I had been so devalued that it didn't matter how I was treated, but that Alan could have caused such suffering to my son was too much and my daughter, son and I never went back to Alan after we left the hospital.

Not long after this I was invited to join the Freedom Programme, a domestic abuse education programme, and it changed my life. I learned that Alan's treatment of me wasn't because of his bad childhood, or his depression, or because he couldn't help it. He *chose* to abuse me because he believed I was inferior, that he owned me, that as a woman I deserved to be treated in whatever way he chose.

It was then I became a feminist.

(http://www.freedomprogramme.co.uk/)

Contributor biographies

Susie Hogarth is an illustrator and writer. She has published a book called 'Hogarth's Very Large Handbook of Celebrity' and has a range of greetings cards. She has also illustrated books, theatre sets and the problem pages of the Erotic Review.

http://www.susiehogarth.co.uk/

Laurie Penny is a writer and feminist activist. She has written for her own blog, the Guardian, the Independent, and is a contributing blogger for the New Statesman. She has published two books.

Deborah Withers is a writer and researcher who exists in between different worlds. In recent times she has set up a publishing company (www.hammeronpress.net), curated an exhibition about Feminism in Bristol in 1973-1975 (http://sistershowrevisited.wordpress.com) and published numerous academic articles. Read more at www.debi-rah.net

Marta Owczarek runs the blog
http://womenfiredangerousthings.blogspot.com

Carrie Dunn is a journalist. She has written for publications including the Times, the Guardian, the Independent and the Daily Express, and blogs at The F Word. She is the author of A Brand New Bright Tomorrow: A Hatter's Promotion Diary, and contributing author to Illuminating Torchwood: Essays on Narrative, Character and Sexuality in the BBC Series. She lectures in journalism and media at various universities, and is currently completing her PhD thesis entitled 'The experience of female football fans in the English professional game: a qualitative study'. If she's not at some kind of sporting event, she's likely to be at the theatre, in a karaoke bar or playing World of Warcraft.

Hannah Mudge was born in 1984. She is based in Cambridgeshire, works in publishing by day and fills the rest of her time with writing, blogging and activism, somehow finding time to hang out with her husband, go running and work on her allotment. Hannah has particular interest in the relationship between the media and gender equality, ending violence against women and girls and the intersection of feminism and religion. She blogs at www.ontoberlin.blogspot.com and tweets as @boudledidge.

Helen Mott has been an active feminist all her adult life and has been involved with the Fawcett Society for most of that time, having been Vice Chair of Fawcett nationally as well as setting up Bristol Fawcett and acting as its co-ordinator since 2001. Bristol Fawcett is an activist group seeking to raise awareness and campaign for gender equality locally. Helen is also a member of many other local and national feminist organisations and groups.

Kat Williams is a co-founder of Swansea Feminist Network.

Marina Strinkovsky writes the blog www.notazerosumgame.blogspot.com.

Jan Martin is a feminist activist and artist. http://www.janmartin.co.uk/

Lucy Jones is a teacher at Edgehill University.

Matt McCormack Evans was born in 1988 and is a feminist campaigner and activist. He is the co-founder and Project Coordinator of The Anti Porn Men Project. He has also worked for OBJECT, a leading human rights organisation that challenges the sexual objectification of women, and volunteered for UK Feminista, a new feminist activist organisation. He is currently in postgraduate education at Durham University.

Finn Mackay has been active in the Women's Liberation Movement for over fifteen years, since leaving home as a teenager to live and campaign at a women's peace camp. Finn has a professional background in youth and advice work, most recently managing a domestic violence prevention programme for an education authority; she has degrees in women's studies, gender studies and policy research. She is currently completing a PhD on Feminist activism against violence against women in the UK. Finn is the founder of the London Feminist Network and revived the Reclaim the Night marches in London in 2004. She speaks and writes regularly on women's rights, particularly on violence against women. In 2010 Finn was the individual winner of the Emma Humphreys Memorial Prize, she is a Trustee of the Feminist Archive South, executive member for the Feminist & Women's Studies Association and on the board of Directors for the End Violence Against Women Coalition.

Ray Filar is a writer and a feminist activist. She blogs at http://raytherah.blogspot.com/

Anna Brown co-ordinates the Bristol Feminist Network. She is a feminist and trade union activist. She was an organiser of V-Day in Bristol.

Francine Hoenderkamp founded the Turn Your Back on Page 3 project, which aims to end media pornography.

Jo Swinson is the Liberal Democrat Member of Parliament for East Dunbartonshire. She entered Westminster as Parliament's youngest MP in 2005, and last year became Deputy Leader of the Scottish Liberal Democrats and Parliamentary Private Secretary to Vince Cable, Secretary of State for Business, Innovation and Skills. She chaired the Liberal Democrat campaign for Gender Balance between 2006-2008 was a member of the 2009 Speaker's Conference which looked at ways to increase the number of women and BME MPs. As well as chairing the Liberal Democrat Women's Policy Working Group in 2009 (www.realwomen.org.uk), she co-founded the Campaign for Body Confidence (www.campaignforbodyconfidence.org.uk) in March 2010.

Jane Mornement is a journalist and feminist. She worked in London on some of the UK's biggest magazines before moving to Bristol where she is a magazine editor and a feminist activist.

Nimko Ali is a feminist activist. She co-founded the charity Daughters of Eve which works with young women who have been affected by female genital mutilation.

Shagufta K Iqbal is a Bristol based poet, who has been actively involved in the poetry scene since 2000. She has performed at numerous venues around Bristol including the Old Vic, Arnolfini and Cube Microplex. She has performed at the 2006 & 2007 Bristol Poetry Festivals and was a member of the Bristol team in the Bristol vs. Paris Slam. She has also performed at poetry and slam events in London, Swansea, Bath, and this year's Glastonbury Festival. Since studying Poetry and Creative Writing at Bath Spa University Shagufta has been holding workshops at both Secondary and Primmary schools across Bristol. She is currently a Research Assistant for UK based poetry organisation Poeticize, which provides a platform for artists of different art disciplines. The organisation promotes the incorporation of Poetry with music, media and dance. Shagufta Iqbal is recently published as part of an anthology entitled 'What They Also Did Was....'

Acknowledgements

When I was a teenager and dreamed of being a writer, I used to draft the 'acknowledgements' page of my best-selling future novel. And so now I am writing one for real! Eek!

Of course my first thank you has to be to the women and men who took the time to write their stories so that they could be collected here. Reading your tales of how you became feminists has been such an inspiring journey for me, and I hope they have inspired you too. Thank you for writing, for sharing, for your honesty and for all the things you do as feminists. You are wonderful writers and people!

Thank you in particular to Debi Withers who's advice and enthusiasm for the project meant I was able to master the complexities of self-publishing and get this book created. I really appreciate your answering my calls and emails, and for showing me the empowering nature of self-publishing.

A big thanks to the wonderful Susie Hogarth for her fantastic cover design which just captures so much of my feelings about feminism. I am so happy to be working with her on this, 6 years after we created our first Crooked Rib zine. She is an amazing artist and wonderful woman.

Thank you to the Guardian for allowing me to reproduce in this book the article 'The Female Eunuch – 40 years on'.

Thanks to Courtney E. Martin and J Courtney Sullivan and the Seal Press for publishing 'Click' and inspiring me to create a UK-based anthology on the story of why we are feminists.

Thank you to my Bristol Feminist Network sisters, especially Nimko Ali, Dr Sue Tate, Jenny Rintoul, Dr Helen Mott and, of course, Anna Brown. I couldn't do any of this without her constant support, love and friendship.

Thanks to Sue as well for lending me the Just Women magazine, and letting me feature some of the stories from there in this book.

Thank you to the feminists of Twitter and the blogosphere for keeping me motivated, uplifted and excited by this incredible movement. BookElfLeeds, Boudledidge, CathElliott, Samira Ahmed, Chitra Nagajararan, Bidisha, Ropes, Steve, Helen G, Incurable Hippy, Lorrie Hearts, NatFantastic, Other Red, Emma Furious, Cath Redfern, Jester, Zohra, TabloidWatch – and the rest.

Thanks to my gang of friends: Emma, Rob, Liz, Liam, Mark, Coz, Sean, Tony, Cat, Nicky and Pip, Chris, Natalie, Julien, Karen, Morvan and the babies. My university friends; Dara, Dave, Doug, Lydia, Anna, Ellie, Rowan, Pete and Joe. And my oldest friends; Kay, Jay, Niz, Holly, Joe, Lawrence, Ralph, Nadia, Emily and Ellie.

Thanks to mum and Kathryn, dad and Louise for raising me a feminist. And Ben too.

Final soppy sentimental thanks to JP. Not only is he an amazing editor, proof reader, photoshopper and tea maker, he is also the most supportive person in the world. I couldn't do half the things I do without his never ending love and support. From activism to writing to making this book, he is always there for me and I love him.

Sorry if I have forgotten anyone.